I0881488

Openings. Onto practices and projects. The genesis of a composition. A plurality of stories. Light suddenly breaking in. A door ajar onto narrative. A day in the fabric of an office. The fruit of meetings with h2o architectes, recounted by Fanny Léglise (author, researcher), with contributions from Miguel Mazeri (anthropologist), Bernard Tschumi (architect) and Frédéric Forte (poet).

2 Openings

Ouvertures. Celles des pratiques et des projets. La genèse d'une composition. Une pluralité d'histoires. Une irruption soudaine de lumière. Une porte laissée entr'ouverte vers la narration. Le jour dans le tissu d'une agence. Une rencontre avec h2o architectes, racontée par Fanny Léglise (auteure, chercheuse), avec les contributions de Miguel Mazeri (anthropologue), Bernard Tschumi (architecte) et Frédéric Forte (poète).

Ouvertures 3

Openings
Fanny Léglise

Fanny Léglise is an architect, PhD student and former editor-in-chief of the journal *L'Architecture d'Aujourd'hui*. Her research focuses on the connections between architectural design and crisis – combining ideas and action – in particular via the bricolage concept developed by Claude Lévi-Strauss. She occasionally teaches in schools of architecture; is a dissertation supervisor at ENSCI-Les Ateliers; and works with institutions, architects and contractors as an author and editorial consultant for the publication of books, articles and competitions. She also participates in the curating of exhibitions and the dissemination of architectural and urban planning culture.

This text is the outcome of conversations with the three associates of the h2o[1] architecture office, Charlotte Hubert, Jean-Jacques Hubert and Antoine Santiard. Addressing a practice that mixes grime and poetry, they explored topics ranging from heritage to the programme, from sites to geometry, from usages to light. Some of the conversations went off in all directions, revealing fresh avenues of exploration; other subjects triggered a gleeful uproar, with a few words or a phrase managing to make themselves heard. Most of all there was an energy. A design dynamic emerged: attentive, permissive, concerned about projects underway and their new inhabitants.

At stake here is architecture, not portraits of architects. A mirror of a raw, sometimes hypersensitive process, of a world apart and a distinctive approach to design. In the course of sometimes disjointed discussions, a set of polarities[2] – complementary contradictions, you might say – took shape. Essential to h2o and indissociable from its members' personalities, these linkages give rise to functional interspaces that gradually flesh themselves out and help guide the office's proliferating activities. The tangible can't be thought through without the intangible, nor matter without the material. The programme challenges the context, intentions spark intuitions (and most definitely vice versa). Permanence is unthinkable without lightness. These collisions form inseparable currents, non-binary electric tensions, and simultaneities, boomerangs and disagreements that are always productive and never reductive.

This has meant deconstructing the vocabulary and attending to nuance. If faced with a choice between two words, opting for the real world. Hunting down the accident, the grain of sand in the works. The bumps to cling to. A bit like Marcel Duchamp's door, open in one direction and closed in the other. What was resolved here (the air current) was challenged there (the art current). An iterative written form taken from among the trio of voices remains the most accurate summing-up of an office turning the page and looking to the future. Where things sometimes hang fire, leaving the door of its cosmos "just barely ajar"[3] and offered to the present.

Attentiveness 66

"Context and its twin, the programme, collide and take issue with each other. Their interaction triggers the office's output, and dialogue begins in a perfectly natural way." The Latin *contextus* means assemblage, unification, unbroken series, and "context" crops up often in architecture, embracing the range of elements making up a site. It goes without saying that it can be historical, patrimonial, physical and geographic – but also economic, social and human. Eminently sensible. The architects at h2o go to context for germination of their projects. The site sends out signals that nourish and give meaning to a given place and time. The architects respond to the context, stripping back its layers in an archaeology of the extant. This is where conception begins, in a reflective conversation with the situation[4]. Induction and interpretation are cultivated simultaneously, following a trail blazed by the act of walking.

The office systematically weighs up the basics, endowing each project with a meaning in the space-time of the question raised. **"Architecture is not a thing that can be removed from its context: no project can be transplanted."** Each new context brings an encounter: terrain unknown or already endlessly crisscrossed; urban, periurban or rural spaces; heritage estates patiently preserved or uglified housing allotments or brownfield sites. To their five senses the h2o team adds a sixth: contact with the territory, attentiveness and "com-prehension"[5] of places. Each conversation is unique, depending on the nature of the situation.

Its grounding in experience means the office has come up with its own methodology, with a compass for keeping its projects on course. It checks out the list of ingredients, both for the site and the programme, collecting, inventorying and mapping them as it goes along. The task could be compared to that of a detective: "You look at things, you look under and through things because they are a source of knowledge, signs of a momentary resourcefulness."[6] Linked to the know-how acquired through work with Historic Monuments, this investigative approach draws on heritage-related skills that it then transposes into contemporary projects. Detailed diagnoses of contexts, surveys of the features and intrinsic virtues of a specific place, archival research: h2o's practice explores traces and layers of usage so as to reveal the palimpsest, grasp its evolution up until the present and better anticipate its future. The project uses description as an essential means of apprehending the world's irreducible complexity. Description is an active part of conception, requiring multiple points of view and representations of the data collected. Markedly influenced by interview techniques and the teaching of social sciences at the school of architecture in Nantes, the h2o associates call on a range of disciplines in their design process, one example being their regular collaborations with Miguel Mazeri, who accompanies them with his slow anthropologist's stride.

Frictions 98

To read a programme is to appraise the merit of the issues raised, the request formulated, and the resultant uses. Site and programme, desires and intentions intermingle and are overlaid. For the initial interconnections the architects employ words as much as drawings. Calmly examining what is being sought, the office looks for the fault line, the interstice out of which the building will be revealed. How to take action without this being perceptible in the margins and interfoldings of the specifications? **"Sometimes evaluating the degree of transformation of a site initially involves deprogramming. Then comes a reprogramming based on the site's uses and meaning."** Patient description culminates in the development of scenarios founded on realistic, feasible hypotheses given formal expression in the drawing of envisaged situations: "Where the map cuts up, the story cuts across... It establishes an itinerary (it 'guides') and it passes through (it 'transgresses')."[7] Stories are overlaid on encounters, readings and observations. Fictions released by representation multiply intentions and make things happen, their different versions ramifying as rhizomic ideas.

"None of the ideas put forward receive immediate recognition. Our projects develop gradually out of variations. The answers lie unobtrusively in the options that have been grafted onto one notion, subtracted from another, added to a third that doesn't line up with the fourth." h2o prefers combination to confrontation. A chain reaction begins, triggered by the urge to write a good story, the right story. Trial and error is part of the process. Working iteratively lets you come up with a coherent whole that's stronger than just the sum of the constraints of a programme and a site.

Imagining and designing a space doesn't mean you've created a place. Place has to be faced up to, used, inhabited. For h2o, to be an architect is to create place. Even if space rhymes too easily with place, it's the inhabiting that counts. The topological supplants the topical. Place is to space as architecture is to construction. "The history of place is brought to life by our experience of it"[8] and for h2o a place is a space with a history. Either that history already exists or it has to be created – or tweaked, going sometimes against the fashion grain. To take an interest in a place is to use it to make other places that chime with the sensory experience and the imaginative realm found there: "I have developed the habit of calling the snippets of things or events that appear before my eyes 'glimpses'. They never last very long. Slivers, splinters of the world, flotsam and jetsam that come and go."[9] Designing involves homing in on some of them.

Representing

"Intuition is an idea that hasn't (yet) found its wording. Drawing makes it evolve. Each drawing allows a move from one idea to another. Like something noted down in its simplest form, the idea is given concrete expression via the hand. Some ideas or doubts can become obsessive unless brought to life on paper. The rough drawing is bare, crude and reductive, and does not always reflect the intended level of complexity. At times clumsiness of line unexpectedly reveals an idea, most often conveying it clearly and forcefully." In the notebooks the projects intersect, disappear and reappear, page after page. Some shapes are like recurring signs, pointers to intuitions.

Drawing lets you collect all sorts of things: people, places, uses, heritage, stories, directions, topography, sense data. The act of drawing sets the project in motion, tells the current story, seeks and communicates: "This pictorial approach to drawings means... that each drawing 're-acts'; it does not simply convey a preconceived idea but provides, on the contrary, an opportunity to do conceptual work."[10] The sketch is a means of transmission. Drawing can be a reciprocal process, the work of several hands. The sketches are sent back and forth and the others respond in a reciprocal goading-on. h2o architectes are not developing any specific aesthetic: handsome drawings have nothing to do with the conception or quality of a project. Drawing is an instrument of production rather than seduction. Out of context it has no visual value; it is simply a trace of what will maybe come about. Sketchbooks and computer files accumulate ideas and capitalise intuitions, helping you not to lose the thread and to be able to backtrack at any moment.

Drawing plays on design. The sketch shapes and articulates images underpinning a concept, i.e., a project strategy. Representation involves several points of view. The sketch gradually becomes more and more detailed, while at the same time the project design becomes simpler. h2o cultivates a taste for technical representation, for drawing that shows its interconnections and constructionnal implementation – its muscles and ligaments. The sketch is never left to its own devices: next to it is the text, generating tension or interaction. Annotating the graphics. The office is fond of metaphors and borrowings from other lexicons: botany, cuisine, physics, chemistry and any number of disciplines. **"Breeding ground, germination, incorporation, fermentation, ingredients, crystallise, transplant"** – a vocabulary that can take some sorting out. Maybe this is where the linkages come from, a way of breaking free of the hackneyed architecture-speak of today's big projects, which nobody takes the trouble to challenge anymore.

126

Complexity

"When our projects reach the point of being too intricate, we have to simplify in the interests of appropriateness and clarity." Resort to 3D models – real or virtual – provides scope for handling and orchestration, in particular of emptiness and its interspaces. "There's another dance happening at every moment, every second, which is the space between bodies. This emptiness, this space between the dancers, intrigues me: an implicit dance whose tension and movement are completely integrated into the overall dynamic and magic."[11] This utilisation of volume generates the tension that the project goes to for its impetus. For its embodiment in the implicit dance of what is coming about.

Volume comes accompanied by distortions, manipulations and confrontations. A new way of addressing things. Each architect chips in in their own way, pushing things to the outer limit, the point of exhaustiveness. And they stand up for this arduousness. Tinkering and gradual command on the one hand, a project achieving autonomy on the other. Imperfections are trimmed back. This is the moment of choices and clarifications. **"We do our best to cultivate generosity and not slide into desiccation, just as we do everything possible to ensure the right accidents."** There is no architecture "without event, without activity, without function; architecture must be thought of as the combination of spaces, events and movements, without precedence or hierarchy between these terms."[12] Antoine Santiard and Jean-Jacques Hubert, both of whom trained in Bernard Tschumi's office, have maintained this attentiveness to the event and its deployment as scores, collages and montages. This may have been their first experience – they would later elaborate on it in their own way at h2o – of joint thinking made of spaces and events, vectors and envelopes.

"Combining knowledge with know-how and purpose, and with experiment and intuition, allows us to compose and associate rather than impose and enforce." This is where doubt really comes in: "Scientific doubt is expressed in analysis, artistic doubt is expressed in action."[13] Doubt can be cultivated. Somewhat abruptly inquiry (analysis) was dropped in favour of doing (action), with no preconceptions. Out of this the office has drawn an equilibrium between use and form, old and new, an inventory and doing thinks. It has never gone for the quick fix, the readymade solution; on the contrary, it lets things deepen, test themselves out, find their place without inducing any immediate response.

160

Dwelling

"Leaving a project open-ended is an elementary form of politeness." By setting up hypotheses and possible directions without creating a hard and fast situation, the h2o team leaves room for the unexpected. Basic needs are supplemented by a "something extra" for those who are going to live or work in the different contexts the office encounters. This means anticipating the way people are going to appropriate a given space, sometimes within the not readily quantifiable boundaries between programme and use – leaving a breeding ground as spontaneously fertile as possible. What falls within the province of the programme and that of architecture? This is the tricky line the agency commits to in advance, without laying down any rules. A kind of capital gain hidden away in the nooks and crannies of the city and the specifications, and which leads to taking over public or shared spaces and "microplaces". The project becomes permissive and amenable, spurred on by interspaces, dual uses, complementary situations. Small things, unforeseen programming changes, honing of uses, all adding up to places for living in.

"Dwelling is space's capacity to welcome acts of generosity and attentiveness. By keeping ample scope for future appropriation, our projects open up perspectives of welcome and trigger events. Planning ahead means never trying to deal with all the issues at once. We constantly adapt to the situation, the building process and the economics." The office's delight – its contagious euphoria – is evident when the new occupants arrive. Moving in, taking their first walk around, a fresh eye on things. Where to open the first box? What furniture to bring out, one piece at a time but in what order, trotting them round the room until they find their place, definitive or not? Man "dwells poetically"[14]. The h2o architects don't draw a "habitat"; rather they envisage the preconditions for dwelling, with no dissociation of housing from its involvement in society: "The human being cannot build and dwell, that is to say, possess a dwelling in which he lives, without also possessing something more (or less) than himself: his relation to the possible and the imaginary."[15] The office is looking for the poetic framework for establishing the feeling of dwelling, which it regards as its primary role as architect. How to guide and assist creative appropriation? For the office the answer would seem to lie in multiple ongoing interactions.

Dialogue broadens the range of possibilities and leads to active involvement with occupants, colleagues and other professions. The physical model emerges as a fabulous tool in these encounters, in that it helps with the sharing of references and concerns. It provides, too, a basis for changes of perspective and response to the general interest and the common good. As a transitional object it is fertile ground for germination of ideas and material for discussion. And as an embodied learning experience it can underpin exchanges with residents as to the densification of a site or with other architects in writing the rules for an urban regeneration project. The office also forestalls the dangers of shortcuts by sticking to the principle of long-term discussions and the project's necessary maturation period.

Walking the tightrope

"An architect always has to be one step ahead. To surprise, and even astonish, but also to anticipate. If things get out of hand they have to be realigned with the project, toned down, and adjusted to the public's expectations and the common good." For h2o creation of place demands an overall vision. For her or his associates the architect is a fixative. The practicalities of city-making don't always fit with this commitment to what shapes the public good, so h2o comes up with strategies reflecting a fresh combination of precision craftsmanship and Anglo-Saxon pragmatism. It programmes and prepares areas – within the limits of the initial budget – for later use, undertakes extra sociological and anthropological studies or helps communicate a vision to potential sponsors. So much footwork, so many machinations with the programme order and situations that arise, in order to keep the aims on track.

The clarity of this structuring process means proposals can be developed that are strong enough to evolve without losing their guiding intentions. To achieve this h2o has no qualms about starting out with a broad brush: so the idea will still be there after intervention by the project's different stakeholders; so the architecture will still be present despite the contingencies. The office sees itself as guaranteeing an overall vision hinging on continuous explanation of its approach and demonstration of what its profession is all about: design. **"If we sometimes have to improvise, the starting point is always a musical score."** Anchored in reality, knowledgeable and alert to the heritage, urban and architectural issues at stake, the three associates immerse themselves in the contemporary and in encounters within and outside their own discipline.

Given the three major forces shaping the city today – climate change, big data and informal building – this is no easy stance. Remaining in control while letting the situation evolve freely demands the skills of a tightrope walker, and this is achieved through a realistic approach to complexity and a form of positive resistance: "What we must do is think of the city as a more open system, one that builds up complexity and that we must cultivate rather than simplify."[16] The office is gradually developing expertise in context complexity, working with city planners, clients who support its approach, and partners and tradesmen capable of implementing that approach.

Advancing along this architectural tightrope necessarily requires a balancing pole that wavers between general considerations and a philosophy of building.

208

Coherence

"Space is defined by its use more than by its materiality. Matter comes after material, which is determined by the constructional choice. The project chooses its matter." In the office's output each material is used for what it is in a quest for constructional legibility. The point is to avoid overemphasis on matter or material, in the interests of structural realism, clarity of assemblage and interpretation of space. An unwritten but reassuring rule. At the same time h2o enjoys breaking it, delighting in inventing protocols and then not sticking to them. Geometry is not just an intellectual game: it overlaps with the story, the place and the event. As a means of enhancing a project's uniqueness, h2o often opts for a single material or family of materials to be used from floor to ceiling. This is a search for a potent aesthetic, a kind of raw power. In the wake of the ultra-complex comes subtraction and entrenchment. Via a single material and a single perception the office strives to get to the strictly necessary, the bare essentials. As in a search for a degree zero[17] – for self-evident spatial realities with no need to proclaim "I am architecture".

"With a firm born after the digital euphoria of the 2000s, we've kept a penchant for loquacious optimism despite the crisis facing us." h2o architectes control some of their temptations by concentrating on process rather that the finished object; by trying to associate minimalist decorum with tectonic rectitude. The office's architectural and artistic philosophy is omnipresent: on walls, in language and mentally. It is always a matter of seeking out the right criteria, of drawing on (especially constructional) cultural roots. Well-laden bookshelves are a concentrate and a wellspring of knowledge and know-how. Having established a balance deliberately rendered impervious to the modish, the architects are out to reawaken the "magical" concepts of permanence and materiality and the search for the right way of doing things. The rules return: the envelope is there at the end of the project as the outcome of the establishing of the uses. Area in the sense of dimension is the minimum element in describing a space. Colour is an abstraction that marks out subspaces, volumes and microplaces within an economy of means. Material enhances spatial reality, as do light, framings and views. Emerging from the plan, area becomes three-dimensional.

With construction come the grain and the imperfections. A roughness that can't be dissociated from fineness. On-site, the architects leave their drawing boards behind. They adjust, adapt, interact with the tangible and the occupants. Non-specifics have to be gone into. The actual making is a time for precision. At h2o they like making layouts and jointing patterns. Drawing returns, refining the details of window sills, balustrades and frames. A thoroughgoing philosophy of building. **"It has to be rough to be tough. No detail is included that can't stand up to use and time's wear and tear."** While space is underpinned by geometry, not everything is immediately legible.

In its handling of volume, the building process cuts free of the constructional mode and of matter. Every technical input involves both its physical impact on matter and its power to symbolise or signify; the two facets are inextricably intertwined[18]. A more complex reading of space emerges, like a previously hidden level of architecture.

The invisible

"Architecture underpins an ecology of the invisible grounded in attentiveness. By its very nature our care for the environment is the opposite of demonstrative." Project sustainability and permanence are fundamental concerns at an office whose environmental vision has gradually shifted from technical or technological solutions to more simple methods assenting to the invisibility of certain inputs. Ecology is a systemic, long-term approach. The many facets of permanence proceed as much from the way materials behave over time as from a project's capacity for regeneration of uses. Born in an era of crises – economic, social, ecological – h2o has never known architecture without them. Yet while this translates for the entire profession as a context of austerity entailing fewer commissions, reduced financial means and, no question, fewer freedoms, a paradox seems to be emerging between luxury minimalism and a philosophy of asceticism[19]. The office keeps a close eye on the fragile boundary between a return to basics, with its potential for a fresh start, and an unproductive formal and plastic archaism[20]. Their preference always goes to a fruitful social activism.

"We draw with the weight of the pencil, which commits us to avoiding solutions experience advises against. Building to last calls for evolvable innovation that can be more programmatic than technical." Innovation doesn't hinge on use of a specific material, a particular implementation process or (maybe temporary) emphasis on an individual subject; it has more to do with a spirit of inventiveness coupled with the precise, attentive monitoring of a protocol of experimentation and evaluation. Faced with today's injunctions, the office thinks hard. How to innovate for the future while talking about the present, and how to preserve while remaining open-ended? How to come to terms with the injunction to innovate? Given the challenge to a teleological history of technology and the turn towards progress of uses[21], synchronicity of modes of making becomes possible. This leaves us free to consider revivals of former technologies and the use of forgotten know-how, both of which have potential for innovation.

Two, four or five years later photographer Myr Muratet took a look at the sites shaped by the office, in a series of "living architecture" images. In one of them a graffiti artist is starting a wall painting as two boys watch attentively. In another a DJ is preparing his set for the night to come. These frank illustrations show what the projects become, how they are inhabited, and the effects of time's passing. You often spot the architects in these photos, back on site to sound out a building and take its pulse. **"The architect guarantees a project's ongoing history, working away until it's time to step aside and leave things to a place that will live on after he's gone. Involvement in the history of something kindles humility."**

242 Meaning

"Heritage isn't there solely to be preserved and enhanced; its meaning has to be restored as well. Modify the extant in order to reveal it. Programme the regeneration of its uses and its meaning." Some of the office's projects trigger a singular dialogue with history. This means knowing how to read history and understand its different strata of intervention. Heritage, in the most general sense, is what is handed down. h2o offers a special, cultivated relationship with it, together with a contemporary eye: "Whether ancient or recent, a work of art – a creative work – must be respected as such, for it conveys an idea and a message."[22] Each project generates meaning by creating renewed spaces, at once symbolic and dwelt in on an everyday basis; thus does architecture bring together semantics and symbolism.

While the historian's quest for comprehension is never finished, the architect can put an end to analysis and go into action. Action that has its own continuity and is linked to the site's set of stories. **"All change seeks to give birth to a new whole, at once powerful and coherent. This in a spirit of respect for the extant, rather than in a binary, dualistic confrontation between new and old."** The office's work touches on heritage, curls up with it, takes it on so as not to enshrine it. Seeks to avoid "the greatest criticism one can make of the many attempts to interpret man's past is that they project onto the visual world of the past the structure of the visual world of the present."[23] h2o architectes investigate the spatial qualities of endlessly modified places, suggesting alternatives to the shortcuts and obvious ideas that would set the restored monument alongside the new intervention. In its emphasis on connection, the office redefines on the basis of traces of time, with no flag-waving. It does not replace the disappearance of the monument and its meaning with promotion of the sign or discourse[24].

In history's long, long time span, architects are only passing through: "[The] approach is long-term because it considers the past, the extant, the unsaid as the grid for the new project, which is only a moment in history and will continue to evolve without us."[25] Projects emerge via contaminations and rebounds, via intersecting rationales and impromptu encounters. Sometimes the office opts for the playful and the unsightly, falling back on clumsy but crafty "pachyderms", not very sophisticated, but relevant and useful in conceiving, weighing up and developing. These odd notions have become essential gradients for h2o practice – a kind of exotic aesthetic[26]. A way of cultivating the pleasure of design, of distancing passing time and the unending world; of finding a role for the designer which brings with it – sometimes against all expectations – a keenly offbeat narrative dimension.

270 Latitudes

"We don't put too much affect into a project. Our approach is an oscillation between the commitment that ensures direction and the trust that leaves elbow room." The architect might be in charge, but he also has responsibilities. At the junction of a network of interdependencies, he is surrounded by a host of participants, is backed up by the transversal skills at his disposal and is sometimes under pressure in his professional encounters. An architect is never alone. Mapping the complexity of interactions both inside and outside agencies makes it clear that "the architectural object is fashioned and transformed in negotiations between multiple stakeholders with different interests."[27] In the transformation of a territory and its uses, each participant is permanently caught up in a convoluted network in which h2o is striving for a place. One that could be achieved stylishly.

The profession of architect seems to be among those which have evolved the least down the centuries. Nonetheless, since the coming of the new millennium, it has had to adapt to contemporary challenges and crises. The three founders have teaching experience in schools of architecture, universities and Columbia University's Paris programme, and as students had already participated in building and educational activities in their schools[28]: "It is inevitable that the work you do as an architect should serve as the point of departure for your teaching."[29] h2o's architects provide criteria for students shaping their philosophy and teach them how to construct a personal work process. Trial and error is learnt, just like representation and programming. Transmission induces challenge and provides a break for reflection far from the fiendish pace of the projects.

"Starting out with no competitions and relying on direct commissions, we've acquired the habit of justifying ourselves. Of explaining and reassuring, demonstrating our hypotheses and being ready to see part of each project up for discussion." Aware that there's no readymade answer to a question involving space, and that there's never just one solution, the h2o team have made the educational an everyday concern. Rather than guides, they see themselves as catalysts influencing the speed of reaction to their work. Each of them functions as a translator between different worlds, a mediator between disciplines, honing her or his vocabulary and speaking skills, and finding the right lexical framework for the project. There's a permanent linguistic quest going on here: getting an ongoing project across to your collaborators, talking to architecture students, adapting your discourse to clients and the construction workers on the site. While it's relatively simple to present an executed work in a meeting, it's a more complex matter to talk about a work in progress. The office doesn't believe in the black box designer-magician[30] and is ready to accept the temporary lack of an overview or not know what the ultimate goal is, so as to take a chance presenting processes or some untreated material or a current practice. h2o has come to terms with complexity, "putting the stories together in an unplanned way... to suggest that all things – stories, incidental sounds from the environment, and, by extension, beings – are related."[31] As we study the office's character, without simplifying, systematising or idealising it, it stands revealed in all of its material diversity and its depth, beauty and strangeness. These are its intrinsic qualities.

h2o was founded in 2005 by Charlotte and Jean-Jacques Hubert. Antoine Santiard joined them in 2008, the year the office took out the Nouveaux Albums des Jeunes Architectes et des Paysagistes award. In 2014 it received the Europe 40 under 40 prize. Charlotte Hubert graduated from the Paris-Belleville National School of Architecture in 1999 and the École de Chaillot centre for advanced heritage studies in 2003. Since 2016 she has been Chief Architect at France's Historic Monuments Department. Jean-Jacques Hubert graduated from the National School of Architecture in Nantes in 1999. Antoine Santiard graduated from the École Polytechnique Fédérale in Lausanne in 2001.

1 The office's name doesn't refer to water.
2 Phrase coined by Yves Citton, professor of literature and media.
3 Gaston Bachelard, *The Poetics of Space*, trans. Maria Jolas (New York: Penguin Books, 2014).
4 Donald A. Schön, *The Reflective Practitioner: How Professionals Think in Action* (New York: Basic Books, 1984).
5 "Comprehension means identifying all the most uniquely economic inter-relationships of the focal point entities involved." Richard Buckminster Fuller, *Operating Manual for Spaceship Earth* (Zurich: Lars Muller, 2008 [1968]), p. 94.
6 Irénée Scalbert and 6a architects, *Never Modern* (Zurich: Park Books, 2015).
7 Michel de Certeau, *The Practice of Everyday Life*, trans. Steven Rendall (Berkeley: University of California Press, 1984).
8 Peter Zumthor and Mari Lending, *A Feeling of History* (Zurich: Scheidegger & Spiess, 2018).
9 Georges Didi-Huberman, *Glimpses*, European Graduate School Video Lectures, 2015.
10 Richard Serra, *Writings/Interviews* (Chicago: University of Chicago Press, 1994).
11 Choreographer Angelin Preljocaj in conversation with h2o.
12 Bernard Tschumi, quoted by Nadine Labedade on the website of the Val de Loire Regional Contemporary Art Collection (FRAC), where Tschumi's models are held.
13 Asger Jorn, "Discours aux pingouins" (Speech to the Penguins), *Cobra,* no. 1, March 1949.
14 A reference to a late poem by Friedrich Hölderlin that begins "In lovely blueness blooms the steeple". See the essays "Building Dwelling Thinking" and "...Poetically Man Dwells..." in Martin Heidegger, *Poetry, Language, Thought*, trans. Albert Hofstadter (New York: Harper, 1971).
15 Henri Lefebvre, *The Urban Revolution*, trans. Robert Bononno (Minneapolis: University of Minnesota Press, 2003).
16 Sasskia Sassen, Ricky Burdett and Richard Sennett in the documentary film *The Quito Papers: Towards an Open City* (2018), produced by Theatrum Mundi (London School of Economics), New York University and UN-Habitat, and directed by Dominick Bagnato and Cassim Shepard.
17 Roland Barthes, *Writing Degree Zero*, trans. Annette Lavers and Colin Smith (New York: Hill and Wang, 1968).
18 Pierre Lemonnier, in Bruno Latour & Pierre Lemonnier (eds.), *De la préhistoire aux missiles balistiques. L'intelligence sociale des techniques* (Paris: La Découverte, 1994).
19 Pier Vittorio Aureli, *Less is Enough: On Architecture and Asceticism* (Moscow: Strelka Press, 2014).
20 This notion harks back to the symposium "The Potentials for the Archaic Today", organised by the Gerphau Research Laboratory and the Paris-La Villette National School of Architecture at the Cité de l'Architecture et du Patrimoine in Paris in June 2018.
21 See David Edgerton, *The Shock of the Old: Technology and Global History since 1900* (Oxford: Oxford University Press, 2007).
22 Pierre Prunet and Nicolas Detry, *Architecture et restauration. Sens et évolution d'une recherche* (Paris: Éditions de la passion, 2000).
23 Edward T. Hall, *The Hidden Dimension* (New York: Anchor, 1969).
24 Henri Lefebvre, *Toward an Architecture of Enjoyment*, trans. Robert Bononno (Minneapolis: University of Minnesota Press, 2014).
25 "Tout est paysage, une architecture habitée. Projets et réalisations de Simone et Lucien Kroll", exhibition from 3 June to 14 September 2015 at the Cité de l'Architecture et du Patrimoine in Paris.
26 Katharyn VanSpanckeren on Edgar Allan Poe, *Outline of American Literature* (United States Information Agency, 2012).
27 Pierre Chabard and Marilena Kourniati, "L'architecture en action, entretien avec Albena Yaneva", in *Criticat*, no. 7, 2011.
28 Just after graduating from the École Polytechnique Fédérale in Lausanne, Antoine Santiard, together with Jacques Cadilhac, Cédric Cornu and Christophe Poussielgue, launched the *e2 contest*, the first international architectural competition on the Internet. 350 teams from 45 countries responded to the theme of the Urban In-Between, with projects that were brought together in the book *e2 Contest: Exploration of the Urban Condition* (2002) and shown at the Pavillon de l'Arsenal in Paris, the São Paulo Biennial, the École Polytechnique Fédérale in Lausanne and La Cambre in Brussels. Then studying at the National School of Architecture in Nantes, Jean-Jacques Hubert, Bertrand Aubry, Stéphane Corbel and Rodrigue Goulard got together as the association Notice. They showed works by students on the medinas in Tunisia and models of the spatial structures of Robert Le Ricolais; organised talks by architects including the Dutchman Wiel Arets; took part in competitions like Europandom – Living in the French Tropics –, and Like a Fish in Water, dealing with urban accessibility in Venice.
29 Herman Hertzberger, *Lessons for Students in Architecture* (Rotterdam: nai010 Publishers, 2013 [1991]).
30 As cultivated by designer John Christopher Jones.
31 John Cage, *Silence: Lectures and Writings* (Middletown: Wesleyan University Press, 1961).

On the walls of the h2o offices in Paris, all sorts of references: Aérolande's light, modular, demountable shelters; Aubert, Jungmann and Stinco's inflatable, self-supporting structures; the Imaginist Bauhaus/Guy Debord; plus Yona Friedman, Gordon Matta-Clark, Kisho Kurokawa, Guy Rottier and his pisé house, Superstudio – and the list goes on...

Sur les murs de l'agence h2o à Paris, un ensemble de références, parmi lesquelles Aérolande – des abris légers modulaires et démontables –, les structures autotendantes gonflables de Aubert, Jungmann et Stinco, le Bauhaus Imaginiste/Guy Debord, Yona Friedman, Gordon Matta-Clark, Kisho Kurokawa, Guy Rottier et sa maison en pisé, Superstudio...

CAPSULE
黒川紀章の作品
PLACE DU FAMILISTÈRE

Ouvertures
Fanny Léglise

Fanny Léglise est architecte, doctorante et ancienne rédactrice en chef de la revue *L'Architecture d'aujourd'hui*. Ses recherches portent sur les relations entre conception architecturale et crises, renouant ainsi penser et faire, notamment à travers la notion de bricolage développée par Claude Lévi-Strauss. Elle enseigne ponctuellement en école d'architecture et est directrice de mémoires à l'ENSCI-Les Ateliers. Auteure et consultante éditoriale, elle collabore auprès d'institutions et de maîtrises d'œuvre et d'ouvrage à la publication de livres, articles et concours, au commissariat d'expositions et à la diffusion de la culture architecturale et urbaine.

Ce texte est le fruit d'entretiens avec les trois associés de l'agence d'architecture h2o[1], Charlotte Hubert, Jean-Jacques Hubert et Antoine Santiard. En évoquant leur travail entre cambouis et poésie, ils ont exploré de nombreux thèmes, du patrimoine au programme, des lieux à la géométrie, des usages à la lumière. Certains échanges ont dérivé librement, révélant de nouvelles pistes d'interrogation. D'autres sujets ont provoqué une joyeuse cacophonie d'où ressortait une phrase, quelques mots dits un peu plus haut. Avant tout, une énergie. Une dynamique de conception s'est dévoilée, attentive, permissive, bienveillante vis-à-vis des projets en devenir comme de leurs nouveaux habitants.

Il est question ici d'architecture et non de portrait d'architectes. Le reflet d'une fabrication brute, parfois écorchée, d'un monde et d'un mode de conception. En sautant parfois du coq à l'âne, un ensemble de polarités[2] – comme des contradictions complémentaires – s'est structuré au fil des discussions. Essentiels à h2o, indissociables des personnalités fondatrices, ces couplages instaurent des entre-deux opératoires qui s'étoffent au fur et à mesure et guident dans le foisonnement de l'agence. Le matériel ne peut se penser sans immatériel, ni la matière sans matériau. Le programme met le contexte au défi, les intentions provoquent des intuitions (et l'inverse est tout aussi vrai). La pérennité ne peut s'imaginer sans légèreté. Ces collisions forment des courants inséparables, des tensions électriques non binaires, des à-la-fois, des rebonds, des « dissensus[3] » porteurs et jamais réducteurs.

Il a fallu déconstruire le vocabulaire, naviguer entre les termes. Entre deux mots, choisir le monde. Chercher le grain de sable et l'accident. Les aspérités auxquelles s'accrocher. Un peu comme avec la porte de Marcel Duchamp, ce qui se ferme d'un côté s'ouvre de l'autre. Ce qui se résout ici (le courant d'air) interroge là (le courant d'art). Une écriture itérative, prise entre les voix du trio, reste la façon la plus fidèle de rendre compte de cette page de l'agence qui ferme l'advenu pour s'ouvrir vers demain. Et se suspend parfois, laissant entr'ouverte[4] la porte de son cosmos, offerte au présent.

67

Attentions

« Le contexte et son pendant, le programme, entrent en collision, en friction. Se frottent l'un à l'autre. Leur interaction active la production de l'agence : un dialogue s'ouvre naturellement. » *Contextus* signifie assemblage, réunion, enchaînement. Le mot « contexte » est fréquemment employé en architecture. Il désigne l'ensemble des éléments reliés à un site. Si le contexte est évidemment historique, patrimonial, physique et géographique, il est aussi économique, social, humain. Éminemment sensible. Les architectes de h2o enquêtent dans le contexte pour faire germer leurs projets. Le site fait signe, ces signes nourrissent, donnent du sens en un lieu et un temps donnés. Ils lui répondent, effeuillent ses couches, pratiquent une archéologie de l'existant. Ici commence la conception, dans une conversation réflexive avec la situation[5]. Induction et interprétation se cultivent simultanément, selon un chemin qui se détermine par la marche même.

L'agence pense toujours à l'assise, conférant à chaque projet un sens dans ce lieu-ci et à ce moment-là. **« L'architecture n'est pas un objet que l'on peut sortir de son contexte : aucun projet ne pourrait être transplanté ailleurs. »** Chaque nouveau contexte est l'occasion d'une rencontre – terrains inconnus ou cent fois arpentés, espaces urbains, périurbains ou ruraux, domaines patrimoniaux patiemment préservés ou sites pavillonnaires malmenés, friches... Les architectes de h2o y emploient leurs cinq sens, et un sixième, celui du contact avec le territoire, de l'attention particulière, de la « com-préhension[6] » des lieux. Chaque conversation est unique, selon le caractère de la situation.

Riche de ses expériences préalables, l'agence a développé une manière de faire, une boussole pour garder le cap des projets. Elle égraine la liste des ingrédients, aussi bien du site que du cahier des charges, pour les collecter, les cartographier et les inventorier progressivement. Ce travail se rapproche de la pratique du détective « regardant les choses, dessous et à travers, parce qu'elles sont sources de connaissances, se font les signes d'une ingéniosité momentanée[7] ». Cette démarche d'enquête, liée au savoir-faire acquis grâce au travail sur les Monuments historiques, se nourrit des compétences patrimoniales pour les transposer dans des projets contemporains. Diagnostic poussés des existants, relevé des éléments et des qualités intrinsèques d'un lieu, recherches dans les archives : la pratique de h2o superpose traces et couches d'usages pour révéler le palimpseste, comprendre l'évolution d'un lieu jusqu'à son état présent et mieux anticiper son avenir. Le projet passe par la description comme un mode d'appréhension essentiel de l'irréductible complexité du monde. Décrire est une activité de conception. Elle nécessite une multiplicité de regards et de représentations des données prélevées. Marqués par la pratique des entretiens et l'enseignement en sciences sociales de l'école d'architecture de Nantes, les associés s'entourent de champs disciplinaires variés pour concevoir. En témoignent leurs collaborations régulières avec Miguel Mazeri, qui les accompagne de ses (lents) pas d'anthropologue.

99

Frictions

Lire un programme, c'est interroger la qualité de la question posée, de la demande formulée, tout comme des usages qui en découlent.

Site et programme, envies et intentions se mêlent et se superposent. Lançant les premiers couplages, les architectes emploient autant de mots que de dessins. En examinant tranquillement ce qui est demandé, l'agence cherche la faille, l'interstice où l'architecture se révélera. Comment agir sans que cela se sente, dans les marges et replis des cahiers des charges ? **« Évaluer le niveau de transformation d'un site, c'est parfois procéder d'abord à sa dé-programmation. La reprogrammation s'appuie ensuite sur les usages et le sens des lieux. »** Les patientes descriptions aboutissent au développement de scénarios basés sur des hypothèses réalistes et probables, formalisées par le dessin des situations projetées. « Là où la carte découpe, le récit traverse. Il instaure une marche (il "guide"), il passe à travers (il transgresse)[8]. » Les histoires se superposent aux rencontres, aux lectures et aux observations. Les fictions, dégagées de la représentation, démultiplient les intentions et font surgir des événements. Elles se déclinent et se ramifient dans une pensée rhizomatique.

« De toutes les hypothèses émises, aucune ne s'impose immédiatement. Nos projets émergent graduellement, par variations. Les réponses se lovent dans les options qui ont su se greffer sur une piste, soustraite d'une autre, additionnée à une troisième, non linéaire avec la quatrième… » h2o préfère combiner plutôt que confronter. Une réaction en chaîne se met en place, portée par la volonté d'écrire une bonne histoire, une histoire juste. Le tâtonnement fait partie du processus. Travailler de façon itérative permet de formuler un ensemble cohérent plus fort que la simple addition des contraintes d'un programme et d'un site.

Imaginer, dessiner un espace n'est pas encore créer un lieu. Le lieu se pratique, s'habite, se vit. Pour l'agence, être architecte, c'est faire lieu. Si « espace » rime trop facilement avec « surface », avec le lieu, c'est l'habiter qui se déploie. Le topologique remplace le topique. Le lieu serait alors à l'espace ce que l'architecture est à la construction. « L'histoire du lieu devient vivante par l'expérience que l'on en fait[9] », et pour h2o, un lieu, c'est un espace qui a une histoire. Soit elle existe déjà, soit il faut la créer, ou encore la détourner en se plaçant parfois à contre-courant. En s'intéressant à un lieu, il s'agit d'en fabriquer d'autres, en résonance avec l'expérience des sens et l'imaginaire qui s'y déploie. « J'ai pris l'habitude de nommer "aperçues" des bribes de choses ou d'événements qui apparaissent sous mes yeux. Cela ne dure jamais très longtemps. Bribes, échardes du monde, épaves qui vont, qui viennent[10] » ; il s'agit d'en fixer quelques-unes pour concevoir.

Représenter

« L'intuition est une idée qui ne trouve pas (encore) ses mots. La dessiner permet de la faire évoluer. Chaque dessin permet de passer d'une idée à l'autre. Comme une prise de notes réduite à sa plus simple expression, l'idée passe par la main pour prendre corps. Certaines idées ou incertitudes sont obsédantes tant qu'elles ne prennent pas vie sur le papier. Le croquis épuré, fruste et réducteur, ne reflète pas toujours la complexité envisagée. Par moments, la maladresse du trait donne à lire une idée de manière inattendue. Le plus souvent, elle la traduit avec force et clarté. » Page après page, les projets se croisent, disparaissent et réapparaissent. Certaines formes sont comme des signes récurrents, révélateurs d'intuitions.

Dessiner permet de collecter toutes sortes de choses : gens, lieux, usages, patrimoine, histoires, orientations, topographie, données sensibles. L'acte graphique initie le projet, raconte l'histoire en cours, cherche et communique. « L'expérience picturale du dessin signifie que chaque dessin ré-agit, qu'il n'énonce pas une idée préconçue mais qu'il est au contraire l'occasion d'un travail de conception[11]. » Le croquis est un support de transmission. Le dessin peut se faire en croisé, à plusieurs mains. Les esquisses sont envoyées aux autres qui rebondissent, jouent les poils à gratter. Les architectes de h2o ne développent pas une esthétique spécifique. Les beaux dessins ne participent pas à la conception ni à la qualité d'un projet. Le dessin est un outil de production plutôt que de séduction. Hors contexte, il n'a pas de valeur plastique, il est simplement une trace de ce qui sera peut-être. Les carnets et dossiers informatiques compilent les idées, capitalisent les intuitions, permettent de ne pas perdre le fil et de pouvoir (toujours) revenir en arrière.

Le dessin joue avec les desseins. L'esquisse construit et articule des images soutenant un dessein de conception, c'est-à-dire une stratégie projectuelle. Le travail de représentation s'organise selon plusieurs loupes. Le croquis s'enrichit progressivement de détails en même temps que le dessein du projet se simplifie. h2o cultive un goût pour la représentation technique, le dessin qui montre ses attaches, sa mise en œuvre. L'écorché. Le croquis n'est jamais solitaire : à côté, en tension ou en dialogue, le texte apparaît. Il annote la production graphique. L'agence aime les métaphores, les emprunts à d'autres lexiques, botanique, culinaire, physico-chimique, à tous les champs disciplinaires. **« Terreau, germination, incorporer, fermentation, ingrédients, cristalliser, transplanter…** » Le choix du vocabulaire donne du fil à retordre. De là peut-être viennent les couplages, comme une façon de sortir de la terminologie consensuelle des grands projets contemporains, que personne ne prend plus la peine de questionner.

Complexités

« Quand nos projets atteignent un niveau d'intrication trop important, il nous faut les simplifier pour accéder à une forme de justesse, d'évidence. » Le passage par des modèles en volume – réels ou virtuels – permet à l'agence de réaliser la synthèse, de manipuler, notamment le vide, l'espace du vide. « Il y a une autre danse qui se joue à chaque instant, à chaque seconde, c'est l'espace entre les corps. Ce vide, cet espace défini entre les danseurs m'intéresse, une danse en creux, de tension et de mouvement participe complètement à la dynamique, à la magie[12] ». La mise en volume crée cette tension qui permet au projet de prendre sa force. De prendre corps, dans la danse en creux de l'advenir.

127

Avec la volumétrie arrivent les déformations, les manipulations, les confrontations. Une nouvelle manière de se frotter aux choses. Chacun interfère à sa manière, pousse les choses jusqu'au bout, à bout. Les architectes se réclament de cet aspect laborieux. Tritures et maîtrise progressive d'un côté. De l'autre, le projet prend son autonomie. Ce qui est imparfait s'affine. C'est le moment des choix, des clarifications. **« Nous nous efforçons de cultiver la générosité, de ne pas glisser dans l'assèchement. Toutes les dispositions sont prises pour que les bons accidents arrivent. »** Il n'est pas d'architecture « sans événement, sans activité, sans fonction », c'est une « combinaison d'espaces, d'événements et de mouvements, sans préséance ni hiérarchie entre ces termes[13] ». Antoine Santiard et Jean-Jacques Hubert, formés au sein de l'agence de Bernard Tschumi, ont conservé cette attention à l'événement, son déploiement en partitions, en collages, en montages. Ils se sont frottés pour la première fois peut-être à une pensée duelle – qu'ils développeront plus tard et à leur manière avec h2o – faite d'espaces et d'événements, de vecteurs et d'enveloppes.

« Conjuguer connaissances, savoir-faire et intentions avec empirisme, expérimentations et intuitions permet de composer et d'associer plutôt que d'imposer et de soumettre. » Le doute a là toute son importance. « Le doute scientifique s'exprime par l'analyse, le doute artistique s'exprime par l'action[14] ». Il se cultive. L'enquête (l'analyse) est quittée un peu brutalement pour le faire (l'action), sans *a priori*. L'agence y puise un équilibre entre usage et forme, ancien et neuf, inventaire et faire. Elle ne se lance jamais dans l'emploi de solutions d'emblée ou d'architectures toutes faites. Au contraire, elle laisse les choses se creuser, se tester, s'imposer sans induire de réponse.

161

L'habiter

« Laisser un projet ouvert est une forme de politesse élémentaire. » En mettant en place des hypothèses et des orientations sans verrouiller une situation, les architectes de h2o laissent place à l'inattendu. Aux besoins primaires s'ajoute un « plus » offert à ceux qui habiteront, travailleront, vivront dans les contextes variés que l'agence rencontre. Il s'agit d'anticiper la façon dont les gens s'approprieront l'espace, parfois dans des limites difficilement quantifiables entre programme et usage. Laisser un terreau fertile au possible, à l'impromptu. Qu'est-ce qui est du ressort du programme, et de celui de l'architecture ? C'est sur ce fil délicat que l'agence s'engage à prévoir l'occasion sans la déterminer. Comme une plus-value qui résiderait dans les interstices et les replis de la ville et du cahier des charges, qui entraîne à s'emparer des espaces publics ou communs et des « micro-lieux ». Le projet devient permissif et maniable, animé par des entre-deux, des usages doubles, des situations complémentaires. Autant de petites choses, de programmations imprévues, de précisions des usages qui, accumulées, parviennent à faire des pièces à vivre.

« L'habiter, c'est la capacité de l'espace à accueillir générosités et attentions. En ménageant une large place pour l'appropriation future, nos projets ouvrent des possibilités d'accueil et suscitent des événements. Projeter, c'est ne jamais chercher à tout résoudre d'un seul coup. Nous nous adaptons sans cesse à la situation, au chantier, à l'économie. » La joie de l'agence, son euphorie communicative se révèlent à l'arrivée des nouveaux habitants. Leur emménagement, leurs premiers pas dans l'espace, les regards neufs sur les choses. Où déballer la première boîte ? Dans quel ordre découvrir les meubles que l'on promènera un à un, leur faisant faire un petit tour de pièce avant de trouver leur emplacement, définitif ou non ? L'homme « habite en poète[15] ». Les architectes de h2o ne dessinent pas de l'habitat mais projettent plutôt les conditions de l'habiter, ne dissociant pas le logement de sa participation sociale. « L'être humain ne peut pas ne pas bâtir et demeurer, c'est-à-dire avoir une demeure où il vit, sans quelque chose de plus (ou de moins) que lui-même : sa relation avec le possible comme avec l'imaginaire[16]. » L'agence cherche le cadre poétique d'une mise en condition du sentiment d'habiter, considérant que c'est là son rôle premier d'architecte.

Comment accompagner l'appropriation créatrice ? La réponse semble résider pour h2o dans le fait de vivre en permanence dans des interactions multiples. Les concertations ouvrent le champ des possibles, instaurent un travail avec l'altérité, habitants comme consœurs et confrères ou autres corps de métier. La maquette se fait l'outil fabuleux de ces rencontres en aidant à partager références et préoccupations. Elle forme un support de changement de perspective, de prise en compte de l'intérêt général, du bien commun. Objet transitionnel, c'est un terreau pour que les idées germent tout en contenant ce qui peut être soumis à discussion. Portant les efforts de pédagogie, la maquette peut soutenir des échanges autour de la densification d'un site avec ses habitants, comme aider à écrire des règles communes d'édification avec d'autres architectes impliqués dans un projet de renouvellement urbain. L'agence évite le projet en raccourci en gardant comme rempart le temps long des échanges et les conditions de maturité d'un projet.

Funambulisme

« Un architecte doit toujours avoir un coup d'avance. Pour surprendre, étonner, mais aussi anticiper. Si les choses partent trop loin, il faudra les ramener au projet, les calmer, réinjecter les attendus publics, favoriser le bien commun. » h2o se sent responsable d'une vision globale pour créer un lieu. Pour ses associés, l'architecte est un fixateur. Les modalités de faire la ville ne sont pas toujours en adéquation avec cet engagement vis-à-vis de ce qui forme le bien public. L'agence développe alors des stratégies et se réclame d'un nouveau couplage entre artisanat de précision et pragmatisme anglo-saxon. Elle programme et prépare des surfaces – dans le respect de l'enveloppe budgétaire initiale – qui seront exploitées plus tard, engage des études sociologiques et anthropologiques supplémentaires ou s'improvise communicante d'une vision pour du mécénat. Autant de pas de côté, de débordements de commande et de situations pratiqués pour tenir les objectifs.

La clarté des éléments mis en place permet de développer des propositions suffisamment puissantes pour assurer leur évolution sans perdre les grandes intentions. Pour cela, h2o n'hésite pas à dessiner « en gras », à gros traits. Pour que l'idée soit toujours là après le passage des différents acteurs du projet. Pour que l'architecture soit toujours présente malgré les aléas du chantier. L'agence se sent garante d'une vision d'ensemble qui passe par l'explicitation permanente de sa démarche et la démonstration de ce qu'est son métier : concevoir. **« Si parfois nous sommes amenés à improviser, ce sera toujours à partir d'une partition. »** Ancrés dans le réel, érudits, en veille sur les enjeux patrimoniaux, urbains et architecturaux, les architectes de h2o s'imprègnent des questionnements contemporains et favorisent les rencontres dans leur milieu disciplinaire et en dehors. Étant donné les trois forces majeures qui dessinent la ville d'aujourd'hui – changement climatique, *big data* et constructions informelles –, la posture n'est pas évidente à tenir.

Rester maître de la situation tout en lâchant prise demeure une faculté de funambule. Elle s'affirme dans une approche réaliste de la complexité, dans une résistance positive. « Ce que nous devons faire, c'est penser la ville comme un système plus ouvert, qui accumule de la complexité, que nous devons travailler plutôt que simplifier[17]. » L'agence développe progressivement une expertise dans la complexité du contexte, s'entourant d'acteurs de la fabrique de la ville et de maîtrises d'ouvrage qui soutiennent sa démarche ainsi que de collaborateurs et artisans à même de la prolonger. Cette progression sur le fil de l'architecture ne saurait se passer d'un balancier qui oscille entre considérations générales et culture constructive.

209

Cohérence

« L'espace se qualifie par son usage plus que par sa matérialité. La matière vient après le matériau, qui est déterminé par le choix constructif. Le projet choisit sa matière. » Dans la production de l'agence, chaque matériau est utilisé pour ce qu'il est, dans la recherche d'une lisibilité constructive. Il s'agit de ne forcer ni matière, ni matériau, au profit d'un réalisme structurel, de la clarté des assemblages et de la lisibilité de l'espace. Cette règle non écrite rassure. Pour autant, h2o aime la transgresser, se fait un véritable plaisir à imaginer des protocoles pour ne pas les suivre. La géométrie n'est pas seulement un jeu intellectuel, elle se télescope avec l'histoire racontée, le lieu et l'événement. Pour renforcer le caractère d'unicité d'un projet, les architectes ont souvent recours à la monomatière – c'est-à-dire à un matériau unique (ou une famille de matériaux) décliné du sol au plafond, à l'opposé du composite. Ils cherchent en cela une esthétique forte, une puissance brute. Après l'ultra-complexité, vient le temps de la soustraction, du retranchement. Avec une matière et une perception uniques, l'agence essaye de parvenir au nécessaire, à l'essentiel. Comme la recherche d'un degré zéro[18], de spatialités évidentes qui n'aient pas besoin de dire « je suis architecture ».

« Avec une entreprise née après l'euphorie numérique des années 2000, nous conservons un penchant pour l'optimisme bavard alors même que nous sommes confrontés à la crise. » Les architectes de h2o régulent certaines de leurs tentations en se concentrant sur le processus plutôt que sur l'objet fini, tentant d'associer bienséance minimaliste et rectitude tectonique. La culture architecturale et artistique de l'agence est partout, aux murs, aux lèvres, en tête. Il est toujours question de chercher la juste référence, d'aller puiser aux racines de la culture, notamment constructive. Des bibliothèques bien fournies condensent et disséminent savoirs et savoir-faire. Dans une position en équilibre, volontairement étanche à l'air du temps, les architectes cherchent à réveiller les notions « magiques » de pérennité et de matérialité, la recherche du bon geste. Les règles reviennent : l'enveloppe arrive à la fin d'un projet comme la résultante des usages mis en place. La surface est l'élément minimum pour qualifier un espace. La couleur est une abstraction, elle délimite des sous-espaces, des volumes et des microlieux dans une économie de moyens. La matière renforce la spatialité, tout comme la lumière, les cadrages et les vues. La surface sort du plan, devient vivante.

Avec la construction, viennent le grain et les imperfections. Une rugosité indissociable de sa finesse. Sur le chantier, les architectes sortent du travail en chambre. Ils ajustent, adaptent, dialoguent avec le concret et avec les occupants. Il s'agit d'approfondir les indéterminés. La fabrication est un moment de précision. Les architectes de h2o cultivent le goût des appareillages, du calepinage. Le dessin revient, celui des détails raffinés des appuis de baie, des garde-corps, des encadrements. Une véritable culture du bâtiment. **« Il faut que ce soit fruste pour que ce soit robuste. Tous nos détails sont conçus pour résister aux usages, à l'usure du temps. »** Si la géométrie sous-tend l'espace, tout n'est pas pour autant donné à lire immédiatement. L'architecture se libère du mode constructif et de la matière par sa qualité volumétrique. Toute technique employée envisage à la fois sa fonction physique d'action sur la matière et sa puissance symbolique ou signifiante, les deux étant inextricablement emmêlées[19]. Une lecture plus complexe de l'espace apparaît, comme un second degré de l'architecture.

L'invisible

« L'architecture sous-tend une écologie de l'invisible faite d'attentions multiples. Notre soin à l'environnement est anti-démonstratif par nature. » La durabilité et la pérennité de chaque projet sont au cœur des questionnements de l'agence. Sa vision de l'environnement s'est déplacée progressivement, de solutions techniques ou technologiques à des dispositifs plus simples, acceptant que certaines interventions ne se voient pas. L'écologie est une approche systémique, à long terme. Les pérennités sont multiples et procèdent tant de la façon dont les matériaux se comporteront dans le temps que de la capacité d'un projet à voir ses usages se renouveler. L'agence est née avec les crises – économique, sociale et écologique – et n'a jamais connu l'architecture autrement. Si cela se traduit pour toute la profession par un régime d'austérité comprenant moins de commandes, moins de moyens et certainement moins de libertés, un paradoxe semble émerger entre minimalisme de luxe et philosophie du dépouillement[20]. Les architectes de h2o observent attentivement la limite ténue qui sépare un retour aux fondamentaux, porteur de réinvention, de l'archaïsme[21] formel et plastique non opératoire. Ils favorisent toujours l'angle d'un activisme social bénéfique.

« Nous dessinons avec le poids du crayon, ce qui engage à ne pas concevoir des solutions que l'expérience nous conseille d'éviter. Pour construire dans la durée, l'innovation doit renvoyer au long terme, elle peut être programmatique plus que technique. » L'innovation ne procède pas de l'emploi d'un matériau précis, d'une mise en œuvre particulière ou d'une attention (peut-être temporaire) à un sujet singulier. Elle relève plutôt d'un esprit d'inventivité, couplé au suivi précis et attentif d'un protocole d'expérimentation et d'évaluation. Face aux injonctions contemporaines, l'agence s'interroge. Comment innover pour le futur alors que l'on parle du présent, comment préserver, rester ouverts ? Comment se positionner face à l'injonction d'innover ? Avec la remise en cause d'une histoire technique vue sous l'angle du progrès pour observer celui des usages[22], la synchronicité des modes de faire devient possible. Et permet d'envisager des résurgences de techniques et l'emploi de savoir-faire oubliés, qui peuvent se révéler novateurs.

Deux, quatre ou cinq ans après, le photographe Myr Muratet revient sur les lieux façonnés par l'agence avec une série de clichés d'« architecture vivante ». Ici, un graffeur entame une fresque sous le regard attentif de deux jeunes garçons. Là, un DJ prépare son set pour la nuit qui vient. Ces illustrations honnêtes montrent ce que les projets deviennent, la façon dont ils sont habités, les effets du temps qui passe. Il n'est pas rare de reconnaître les architectes dans ces photographies, revenus eux aussi ausculter un bâtiment, prendre son pouls. **« L'architecte est garant de la continuité de l'histoire d'un projet ; il se distingue par sa persévérance jusqu'à ce qu'il doive s'effacer pour laisser prendre les lieux, qui continueront bien après son passage. S'inscrire dans l'histoire de quelque chose pousse à l'humilité. »**

243

Sens

« Le patrimoine n'est pas seulement là pour être conservé et mis en valeur, il faut lui redonner du sens. Modifier l'existant pour le révéler. Programmer le renouvellement de ses usages et de sa signification. » Un certain nombre de projets de l'agence entament un dialogue singulier avec l'histoire. Ce qui oblige à savoir la lire, à comprendre les différentes strates d'intervention qui la composent. Le patrimoine, au sens le plus général, est ce qui se transmet. h2o lui offre un rapport cultivé et privilégié, associé à un regard contemporain. « Une œuvre ancienne ou récente, qui est une œuvre d'art, donc une œuvre de création, doit être respectée en tant que telle car elle est porteuse d'une pensée et d'un message[23] ». Chaque projet fait sens en créant des espaces renouvelés, autant symbole que lieu habité au quotidien ; l'architecture conjugue alors sémantique et symbolique.

Alors que l'historien n'a jamais fini son travail de compréhension, l'architecte peut clore son analyse et passer à l'action. Un acte dans la continuité, en lien avec l'ensemble des histoires qui ont affecté les lieux. **« Toute transformation cherche à donner naissance à un nouvel ensemble puissant et cohérent, dans le respect de l'existant plutôt que dans une confrontation binaire, duelle, entre neuf et ancien. »** Les productions de l'agence touchent au patrimoine, s'y lovent, s'y frottent pour ne pas le sanctuariser. Cherchent à éviter « le reproche le plus sérieux que l'on puisse adresser aux nombreuses tentatives d'interprétation du passé de l'homme : [projeter] sur le monde visuel du passé la structure du monde visuel contemporain[24] ». Les architectes de h2o interrogent la spatialité de lieux maintes fois remaniés, proposent des alternatives aux raccourcis, à une pensée évidente qui ferait se juxtaposer le monument restauré et l'intervention nouvelle. En privilégiant le couplage, l'agence redéfinit à partir des traces du temps, sans gesticulations. Ne remplace pas la disparition du monument et de son sens par une promotion du signe ou du discours[25].

Dans le temps long de l'histoire, les architectes ne sont que de passage. « [L']approche est de longue durée puisqu'elle considère le passé, l'existant, le non-dit, comme la trame sur laquelle se pose le nouveau projet qui n'est qu'un moment dans l'histoire et qui continuera à évoluer sans nous[26] ». Les projets émergent par contaminations et rebonds, intersection de logiques et rencontres impromptues. L'agence joue parfois du ludique et du disgracieux.

Ses replis abritent des « pachydermes », patauds et malins, peu raffinés mais pertinents, qui servent à penser, peser et développer un projet. Ces étrangetés deviennent des gradients essentiels de l'architecture de h2o, comme une esthétique insolite[27]. Une façon de cultiver le plaisir de la conception, de mettre à distance le temps qui court, le monde qui va. De trouver une place de concepteur qui apporte – parfois contre toute attente – une dimension narrative affûtée et décalée.

271

Latitudes

« Nous ne plaçons pas trop d'affects dans un projet. Notre démarche est une oscillation entre s'impliquer pour orienter et savoir confier pour laisser du champ. » Si l'architecte est responsable d'un projet, il est aussi redevable. Placé au carrefour d'un réseau d'interdépendances, il s'entoure d'une multitude d'intervenants, se conforte par les savoirs transversaux qu'il peut faire entrer dans son projet, et se trouve parfois chahuté par la rencontre avec les uns et les autres. Un architecte n'est jamais seul. La cartographie des interactions complexes au sein des agences et au dehors révèle que « l'objet architectural se fabrique et se transforme dans une négociation entre de multiples acteurs ayant des intérêts différents[28] ». Dans la transformation du territoire et de ses usages, chacun est pris en permanence dans un réseau aux résonances multiples dans lequel h2o cherche à trouver sa place. Une place qui peut être prise avec élégance.

La profession d'architecte semble être l'une de celles qui ont le moins évolué pendant des siècles. Elle doit pourtant s'adapter aux défis contemporains et aux crises depuis le début des années 2000. Les trois fondateurs de l'agence ont une expérience de l'enseignement, aussi bien en école d'architecture, à l'université que dans le programme parisien de la Columbia University. Étudiants, ils participaient déjà à la construction et à la diffusion du savoir au sein de leurs écoles[29]. « Il est inévitable que le travail d'un architecte serve de point de départ à son enseignement[30] ». Les architectes de h2o nourrissent les références des étudiants en train de constituer leur culture et leur apprennent à construire un processus personnel. Tâtonner s'enseigne, tout comme représenter ou programmer. La transmission favorise la remise en question, offre des temps de pause pour réfléchir loin du rythme effréné des projets.

« Nous avons pris l'habitude de rendre des comptes dès nos premières commandes, directes, sans concours. D'expliquer et de rassurer, de montrer des hypothèses et, de fait, d'accepter de voir une partie du projet mise en discussion. » Conscients qu'il n'y a pas de réponse toute faite à une question d'espace, ou qu'il n'y a jamais qu'une seule solution, les architectes de h2o érigent la pédagogie en préoccupation quotidienne. Plutôt que guides, ils se voient comme des catalyseurs qui modifient la vitesse d'une réaction à l'œuvre. Chacun se fait traducteur entre différents mondes, traverse les champs disciplinaires, travaille son vocabulaire, ses capacités oratoires et trouve le lexique adapté au projet. Cette forme du langage est une recherche permanente : pour communiquer aux collaborateurs un projet en développement, s'adresser aux étudiants à l'école ou s'adapter aux commanditaires et corps de métier sur un chantier.

S'il est relativement simple de présenter une réalisation en conférence, il est plus complexe de parler d'une chose en train de se faire. L'agence ne cultive pas la boîte noire du concepteur magicien[31] et accepte de ne pas avoir encore de vue d'ensemble ou d'ignorer la finalité d'un projet pour prendre le risque de présenter des processus, une matière brute, une pratique au présent. h2o assume sa complexité et expose « des histoires ensemble de façon non planifiée de manière à suggérer que toutes les choses – histoires, sons provenant d'un environnement, et, par extension, existences – sont reliées[32] ». En observant la nature de l'agence sans la simplifier, l'organiser ou la magnifier, l'hétérogénéité de sa matière, sa profondeur, sa beauté ou son étrangeté se révèlent. Ce sont ses qualités intrinsèques.

h2o a été fondé en 2005 par Charlotte et Jean-Jacques Hubert. Antoine Santiard rejoint l'agence en 2008, année où elle est lauréate des Nouveaux Albums des jeunes architectes et des paysagistes. L'agence reçoit le prix Europe 40 under 40 en 2014. Charlotte Hubert a été diplômée de l'École nationale supérieure d'architecture de Paris-Belleville en 1999 et du Centre des hautes études de Chaillot en 2003. Elle est architecte en chef des Monuments historiques depuis 2016. Jean-Jacques Hubert a été diplômé de l'École nationale supérieure d'architecture de Nantes en 1999. Antoine Santiard a été diplômé de l'École polytechnique fédérale de Lausanne en 2001.

1 Le nom de l'agence ne fait pas référence à l'eau.
2 Selon la définition qu'en donne le professeur de littérature et médias Yves Citton.
3 Selon la définition qu'en donne le philosophe Jacques Rancière.
4 Gaston Bachelard, *La Poétique de l'espace*, Presses universitaires de France, 1970.
5 Donald A. Schön, *The Reflexive Practitioner: How Professional Think in Action*, Basic Books, 1984.
6 Richard Buckminster Fuller, *Manuel d'instruction pour le vaisseau spatial Terre* (1963), Lars Muller Publisher, 2009.
7 Irénée Scalbert et 6a Architects, *Never Modern*, Park Books, 2015, traduction de l'auteur.
8 Michel de Certeau, Luce Giard et Pierre Mayol, *L'Invention du quotidien*, tome I : *Arts de faire*, 1980.
9 Mari Lending, dans un échange avec Peter Zumthor, *Présence de l'histoire*, Scheidegger & Spiess, 2018.
10 Georges Didi-Huberman, *Aperçues*, Éditions de Minuit, 2018.
11 Richard Serra, *Écrits et entretien, 1970-1989*, Daniel Lelong éditeur, 1990.
12 Extrait d'un entretien entre le chorégraphe Angelin Preljocaj et l'agence.
13 Bernard Tschumi, cité par Nadine Labedade, sur le site internet du FRAC Centre qui conserve des maquettes de l'architecte dans ses collections.
14 Asger Jorn, *Discours aux pingouins et autres écrits*, éditions de l'École nationale supérieure des beaux-arts, 2001.
15 Repris d'un poème de Friedrich Hölderlin dans le cadre du colloque « L'homme et l'espace », où Martin Heidegger donne la conférence intitulée « Bâtir habiter penser ».
16 Henri Lefebvre, *La Révolution urbaine*, Gallimard, 1970.
17 Saskia Sassen, Ricky Burdett et Richard Sennett, dans le documentaire *The Quito Papers: Towards an Open City*, produit par le Theatrum Mundi (London School of Economics), New York University et ONU-Habitat, réalisé par Dominick Bagnato et Cassim Shepard, 2018.
18 Roland Barthes, *Le Degré zéro de l'écriture*, Seuil, 1953.
19 Pierre Lemonnier, in *De la préhistoire aux missiles balistiques. L'intelligence sociale des techniques*, sous la direction de Bruno Latour et Pierre Lemonnier, La Découverte, 1994.
20 Pier Vittorio Aureli, *Less Is Enough: On Architecture and Ascetism*, Strelka Press, 2014.
21 L'emploi de cette formule découle d'un échange au sujet du colloque « L'archaïque et ses possibles aujourd'hui » organisé par le laboratoire Gerphau et l'ENSA de Paris-La Villette à la Cité de l'architecture et du patrimoine en juin 2018.
22 David Edgerton, *The Shock of the Old: Technology and Global History since 1900*, Oxford University Press, 2007.
23 Pierre Prunet et Nicolas Detry, *Architecture et restauration. Sens et évolution d'une recherche*, Éditions de la Passion, 2000.
24 Edward T. Hall, *La Dimension cachée (1966)*, Seuil, 1971.
25 Henri Lefebvre, *Vers une architecture de la jouissance* (1973), traduction de la revue *Criticat*, n° 14, 2014.
26 « Tout est paysage, une architecture habitée. Projets et réalisations de Simone et Lucien Kroll », exposition du 3 juin au 14 septembre 2015 à la Cité de l'architecture et du patrimoine à Paris.
27 Kathryn VanSpanckeren à propos de l'œuvre d'Edgar Allan Poe, *Esquisse de la littérature américaine*, publiée par la United States Information Agency.
28 Pierre Chabard et Marilena Kourniati, « L'architecture en action, entretien avec Albena Yaneva », in *Criticat*, n° 7, 2011.
29 Antoine Santiard, avec Jacques Cadilhac, Cédric Cornu et Christophe Poussielgue, lance « e2 contest », premier concours international par internet, à l'issue de son diplôme à l'École polytechnique fédérale de Lausanne. 350 équipes issues de 45 pays ont partagé leurs réponses architecturales sur le thème de l'entre-deux urbain. L'aventure est rassemblée dans l'ouvrage *e2 contest. Exploration of the Urban Condition* (2002) et présentée au Pavillon de l'Arsenal à Paris, à la Biennale de São Paulo, à l'EPFL et à La Cambre à Bruxelles. Alors en troisième année à l'École nationale supérieure d'architecture de Nantes, Jean-Jacques Hubert se réunit avec Bertrand Aubry, Stéphane Corbel et Rodrigue Goulard au sein de l'association Notice. Ils montent des expositions de travaux d'étudiants sur les médinas tunisiennes et de maquettes de structures spatiales de Robert Le Ricolais, organisent des conférences d'architectes, notamment celle du Néerlandais Wiel Arets, et participent à des concours comme Europandom (Europan, habiter la ville outre-mer) et Like a Fish in Water sur l'accessibilité de la ville de Venise.
30 Herman Hertzberger, *Leçons d'architecture* (1991), Infolio, 2010.
31 D'après un schéma du designer John Christopher Jones.
32 John Cage, *Silence: Lectures and Writings*, Wesleyan University Press, 1961, traduction de l'auteur.

31

Invited with several other offices to create houses for the middle of the Moroccan desert, we had the good fortune to be able to design four of them. Made of earth and stone, they had in common a telluric connection with the site, rooted in vernacular architecture and the potency of the desert. For this project we focused our thinking on the concepts of habitability, interiority and protection, which led to spaces sequenced according to different degrees of porousness. Each house creates its own universe via a unique relationship with the courtyard, seen as the specific, privileged interface with the desert.

Avec plusieurs autres agences, nous avons été invités à dessiner des maisons au milieu du désert marocain. Nous avons eu la chance d'en concevoir quatre. Constituées de terre et de roche, elles ont pour point commun leur rapport tellurique au site, en référence à l'architecture vernaculaire comme à la puissance du désert. Pour ce projet, nous avons axé notre réflexion sur les notions d'habitabilité, d'intériorité et de protection. Les espaces sont ainsi séquencés selon différents degrés de perméabilité. Chaque maison fabrique son propre univers en proposant un rapport unique à la cour, vue comme l'interface spécifique et privilégiée avec le désert.

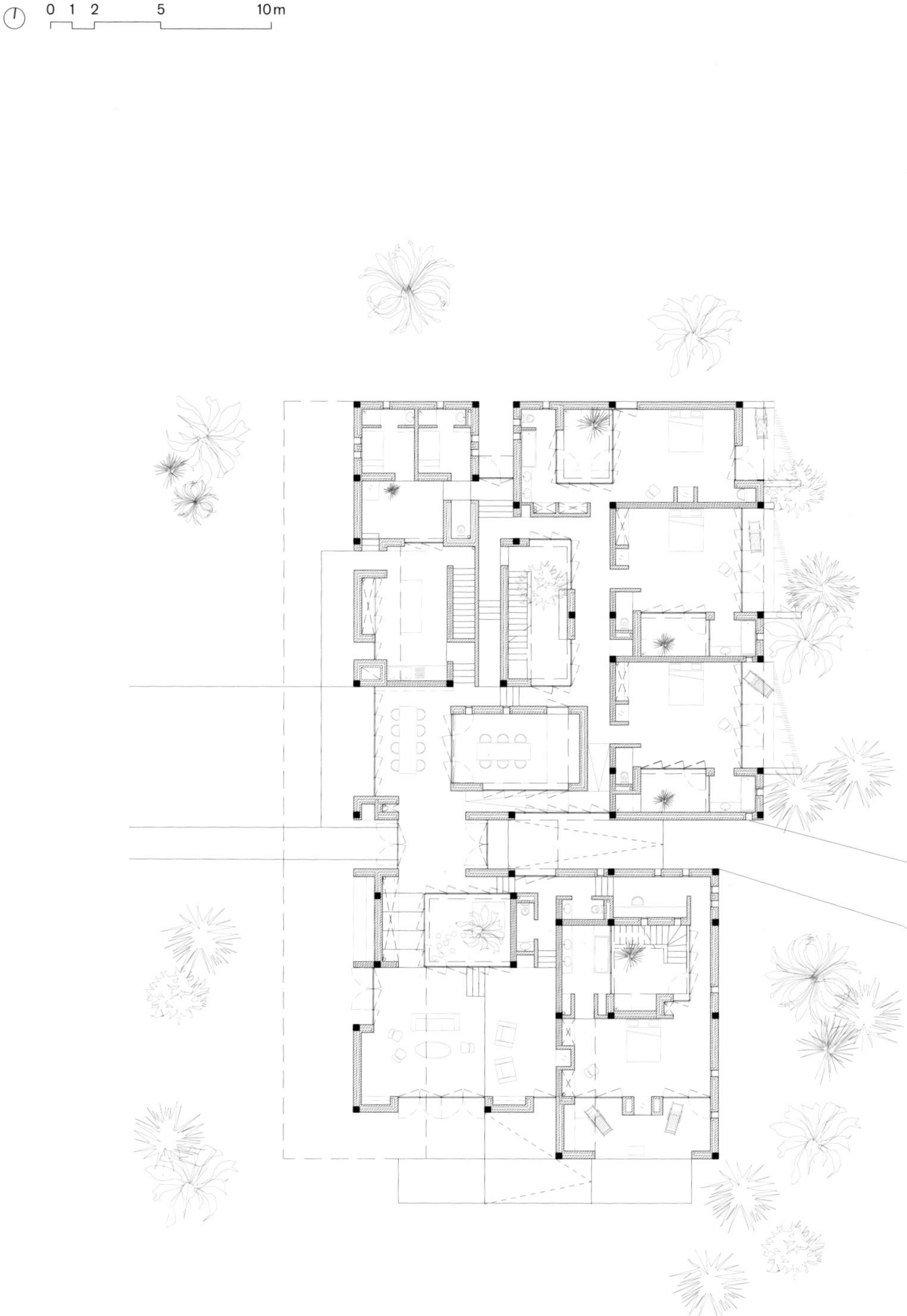
0 1 2 5 10m

Taken out of context, this cast aluminium bollard seems distinctly incongruous. Set in the main courtyard of the French National Assembly as part of a site-specific design, it geometrically punctuates the overall space and delimits the different areas according to their use. The perception of its tapering shape changes in line with its location and the gaze of the passer-by.

Extrait de son contexte, ce potelet en fonte d'aluminium semble un objet incongru. Implanté dans la cour d'honneur de l'Assemblée nationale, sa géométrie ponctue l'espace et délimite les zones en fonction de leur usage, selon un dessin imaginé spécifiquement pour le lieu. La perception de sa forme effilée change suivant son implantation et le regard du passant.

Potelet, Assemblée nationale, Paris

RENFLEMENT.
DUCTAL. 01 11 05
DU MODULE.

JONCTION
ALLER JUSQU'A L'ECHELLE 1
ASSEMBLAGE

This furniture project explores the possibility of designing a minimal, abstract shape that does not dictate how it is to be used – a shape not afraid of being sculptural. What's the narrative identity of this object so far removed from the classical typologies, of a bench liberated from the traditional stipulations regarding formal plausibility and functionality? The seat – ultra high performance fibre reinforced concrete (UHPFRC) – envelops and develops to provide a spatial welcome for the body, while the modular shell, calibrated and fine-tuned to the limit, requires a minimum of material.

Ce travail sur le mobilier explore la possibilité de concevoir une forme minimale et abstraite, non directive du point de vue des usages, une forme qui se permet d'être sculpturale. Quelle est l'identité narrative de cet objet, loin des typologies classiques ? Le banc s'émancipe des conditions traditionnelles, qui allient vraisemblance de la forme et fonctionnalité. L'assise en BFUP (béton fibré à ultra-hautes performances) s'enveloppe et se développe pour accueillir le corps dans l'espace. La coque modulaire s'ajuste et s'affine à l'extrême, employant un minimum de matière.

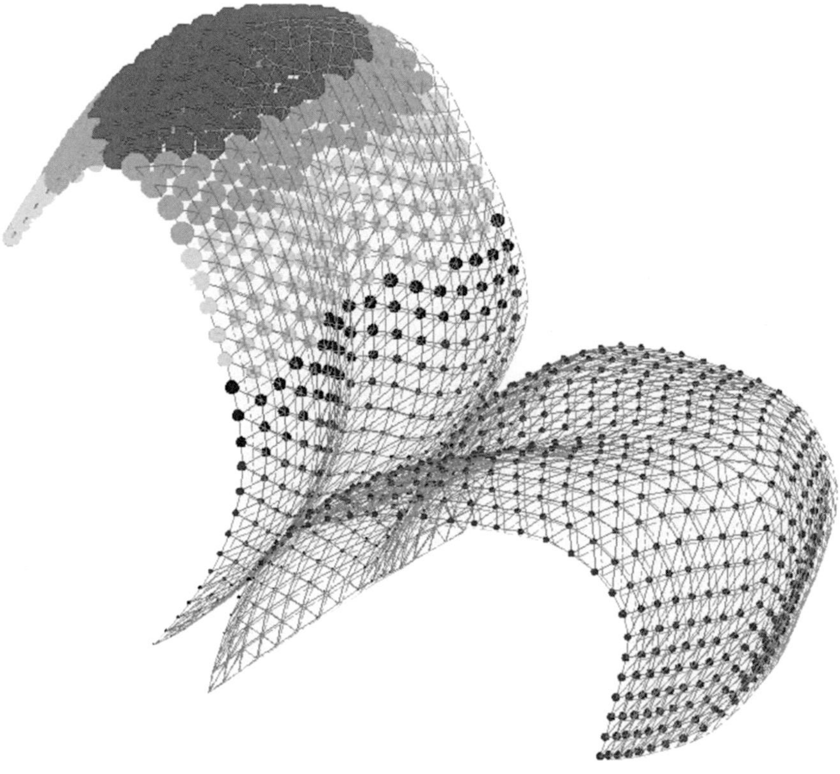

This simple component fits in the hand and is designed to proliferate and multiply. Once assembled, the basic, solid oak shape can become a stool, bench or side table, revealing complex new possibilities in the process.

Cet élément simple, qui tient dans la main, a vocation à proliférer, à se démultiplier. La forme primitive taillée dans du chêne massif, une fois assemblée, peut devenir tabouret, banc ou table d'appoint, révélant de nouvelles complexités.

In 2009 h2o was among the twenty emergent offices selected by the Architects' Directory, published annually by the magazine *Wallpaper**. The magazine asked us to design a house according to a singular architectural requirement: an unspecified context. To avoid the potential excesses of an above-ground project, we came up with a narrative of dual, interacting spaces: a house seen as two intertwining trajectories, one open and the other closed. Void as the upshot of fullness. Crossing of paths enabling different degrees of porousness and permeability. Each space thus becomes specific, each layout generates a particular function.

h2o figure en 2009 parmi les vingt agences émergentes sélectionnées dans l'« Architects' Directory » que publie chaque année le magazine *Wallpaper**. Ce dernier nous a demandé de concevoir une maison selon un exercice singulier en architecture : un contexte indéterminé. Pour éviter les dérives d'un projet hors sol, nous avons imaginé une histoire d'espaces duaux, en interaction. La maison est ainsi conçue selon deux trajectoires qui s'entremêlent, l'une ouverte, l'autre fermée. Le vide apparaît comme la résultante du plein. Le croisement des parcours permet de créer différents degrés de porosité, de perméabilité. Chaque espace devient spécifique, chaque disposition génère une fonction particulière.

john
ston
ACTAR

WILEY
ET ON TUERA TOUS LES AFFREUX
VERNON SULLIVAN
ACTAR

This dual programme – rehabilitation of a former covered market and construction of an office block – is part of the new Pleyel neighbourhood in Saint-Denis. The pre-existing market has a park running through it, which provides osmosis with its surroundings, while the new building, integrated into the urban development programme led by OMA, is helping to revitalise the look of the neighbourhood with a front giving onto the network of railway tracks stretching away to the east. The wooden architecture is structured by traffic cores in the corners, which free up the floor areas and allow total flexibility of use. The ribbed glass envelope generates a host of reflections and offers slanting views while reinforcing the building's overall structural stability.

Ce double programme – réhabilitation d'une ancienne halle et construction de bureaux – s'insère dans le nouveau quartier Pleyel, à Saint-Denis. La halle existante, traversée par un parc, offre une porosité avec son environnement. Le bâtiment neuf, calé dans la trame du projet de développement urbain dirigé par OMA, contribue à donner un nouveau visage au quartier en créant un front bâti ouvert sur le paysage, en l'occurrence le réseau de voies ferrées qui s'étirent à l'est. L'architecture de bois est structurée par des noyaux de circulation reportés dans les angles, qui libèrent les plateaux et permettent une entière flexibilité des usages. L'enveloppe de verre plissée démultiplie les reflets et offre des vues biaises tout en confortant la stabilité structurelle de l'ensemble.

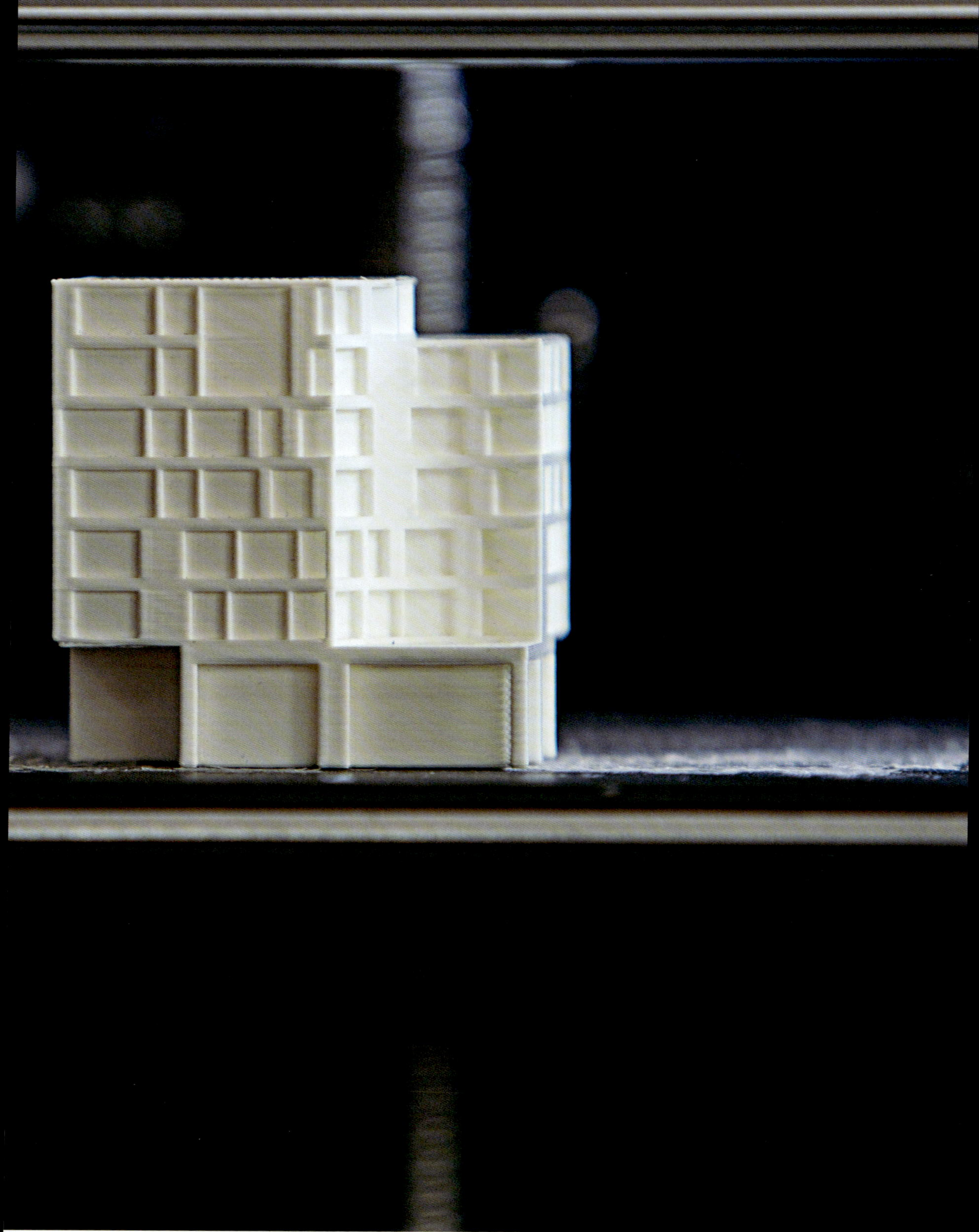

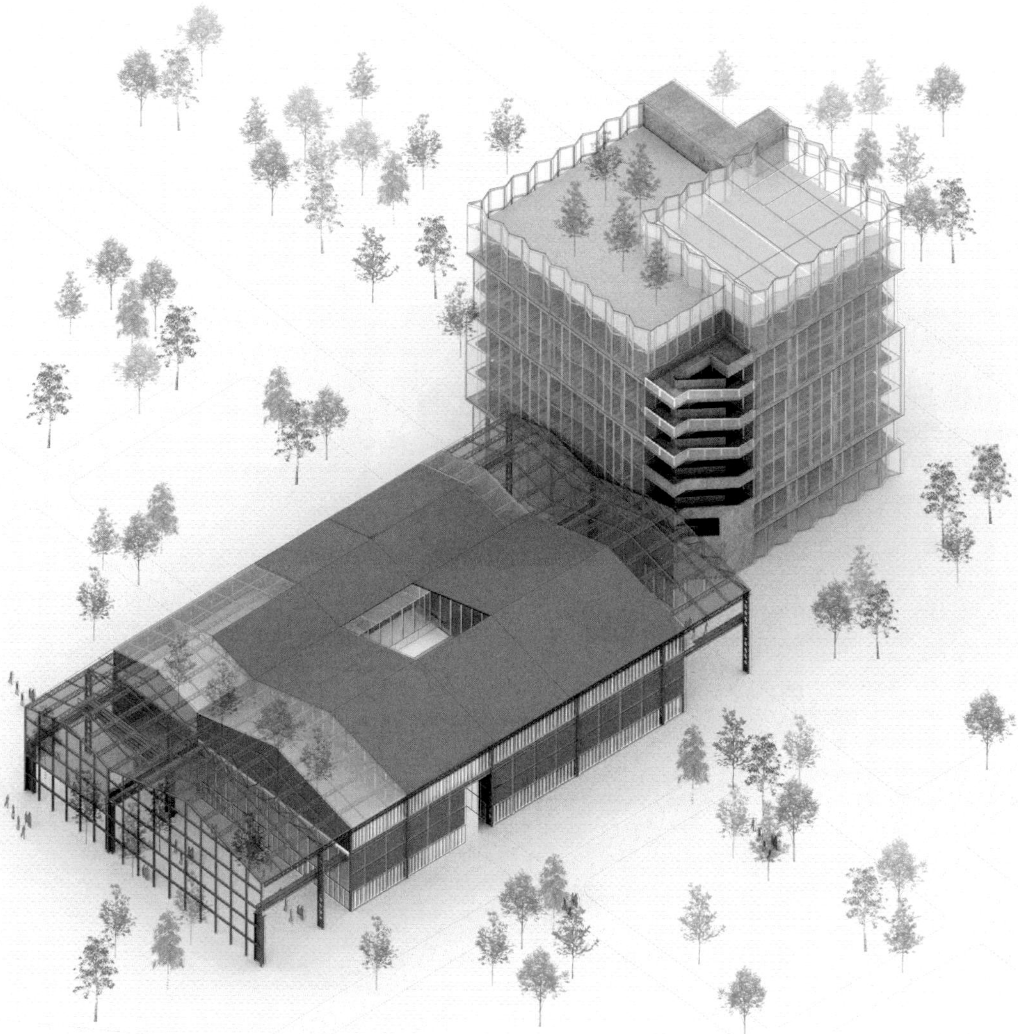

PLAN D'ETAGE COURANT

"Context and its twin, the programme, collide and take issue with each other. Their interaction triggers the office's output and dialogue begins in a perfectly natural way. Architecture is not a thing that can be removed from its context: no project can be transplanted."

« Le contexte et son pendant, le programme, entrent en collision, en friction. Leur interaction active la production de l'agence : un dialogue s'ouvre naturellement. L'architecture n'est pas un objet que l'on peut sortir de son contexte : aucun projet ne pourrait être transplanté ailleurs. »

Summer, heatwave. Small humans clad only in nappies, delighting in the misting of the atomiser. Under the laughing gaze of the kindergarten staff. Incredible the way little kids sleep like logs. A sidelong glance at the bigger ones, to make sure everything's okay. Carrying a baby, stepping over the child who's settled between the rows in an unconscious spatial strategy for keeping interaction going. Misty-eyed kiddywinks watching the backs of daddies setting off to work. Tranquilly ensconced at the corner of the guardrail, bottom set firmly on the concrete step, playing with the plastic cows. Borrowed light through the glass partition, the young woman sterilising the babies' bottles. The contortions of adults sitting on kids' chairs, knees in their faces. And the trucks with their wheels in the air, waiting for tomorrow and the tiny tots' next car race. Safe, sterile spaces, little shoes slipped off, the parents' big plastic slippers. Greenery a little way off: a climbing plant at the entry, dead leaves on the grill. Looking downwards, from the first to the ground floor, from the big girl to the small one. Mirrors. Looking upward, from the baby to the world, parents arriving, about to rediscover their offspring. **FL**

Été, canicule. Petits humains seulement vêtus de couches, ravis sous les fines gouttelettes du brumisateur. Regards rieurs des assistantes maternelles. Incroyable sommeil de plomb des enfants. Coup d'œil de biais, pour veiller au grain, aux grands. Un bébé dans les bras, enjamber celui qui s'est installé au milieu du passage, comme un choix spatial stratégique et inconscient pour toujours rester en interaction. Filtres entre cours, prunelles légèrement embuées des petits bonhommes qui regardent le dos de leur papa parti travailler. Tranquillement installé à l'angle de la rambarde, les fesses bien calées sur la remontée de béton, jeu avec les vaches en plastique. Second jour, par la fenêtre intérieure, vers la jeune femme qui stérilise les biberons. Les positions contorsionnées, genoux au visage, des adultes lorsqu'ils s'assoient sur des chaises d'enfant. Et les camions, roues en l'air, dans l'attente du lendemain, de la prochaine course automobile des tout-petits. Espaces sécurisés et stériles, petites chaussures enlevées, gros sur-chaussons en plastique des parents. La végétation s'installe à distance : sur une treille à l'entrée, avec les feuilles mortes sur la grille. Vision du haut vers le bas, du premier étage au rez-de-chaussée, de la grande vers la petite fille. Miroirs. Du bas vers le haut, du bébé vers le monde, des parents qui arrivent vers leur progéniture qu'ils vont bientôt retrouver. **FL**

Épée de Bois municipal day nursery, Paris

The fabric, glass and steel extension to the day nursery has been slipped into the cramped courtyard of a Paris apartment building, where it connects and interacts with both its built and vegetal environments. The project acknowledges the rights of a tree and height-wise is adapted to the extant moulding. Light and playful, the architecture offers extra uses via new outside spaces and more spacious volumes. The immaculate envelope and generous glazed areas are equipped with filters that direct the light and ensure privacy, while the climbing plants on the trellises anchor the building to the ground.

L'extension de la crèche, en toile, verre et acier, se glisse au fond d'une cour d'immeuble parisienne exiguë. Elle tisse des liens et crée un dialogue avec son environnement, bâti mais aussi végétal. Le projet se plie au droit d'un arbre, s'ajuste en hauteur à la modénature de l'existant ; son enveloppe se soulève pour marquer l'entrée. Cette architecture légère et ludique offre un prolongement d'usages grâce à de nouveaux espaces extérieurs et des volumes plus ouverts. L'enveloppe immaculée et les verrières généreuses sont dotées de filtres qui orientent la lumière et protègent des regards. Les plantes qui grimpent le long des treilles rattachent la construction au sol.

Different country, different continent, different climate. On Santa Teresa's hill in Rio de Janeiro, the Castello is a landmark in its own right. Once abandoned amidst the lush local vegetation, this "château" has been restored and transformed into a residential hotel: fourteen studios, all of them unique, all recreations of the original volumes and decors, all offering different ambiences to residents in the two wings, the attic or the tower. A wealth of species of Brazilian wood present all sorts of tonal variations, depending on colour, saturation and veining. The contrasts between them are heightened by the marked variations in the natural light filtering in through the restored shutters.

Autre pays, autre continent, autre climat. Sur la colline de Santa Teresa à Rio de Janeiro, l'habitation Castello agit comme un repère dans le paysage. Ce « château », abandonné au sein d'une végétation luxuriante, a été restauré pour devenir une résidence hôtelière. Chacun des quatorze studios est unique, s'adaptant aux volumes et aux décors conservés. Les résidents profitent d'ambiances variées selon qu'ils occupent l'une des deux ailes, les combles ou bien la tour. La richesse des essences de bois brésilien a permis de varier les tonalités, en fonction de la couleur, de la saturation et du veinage de chacune. Ces contrastes sont renforcés par les fortes variations de la lumière naturelle, filtrée par des persiennes restaurées elles aussi.

Reformas

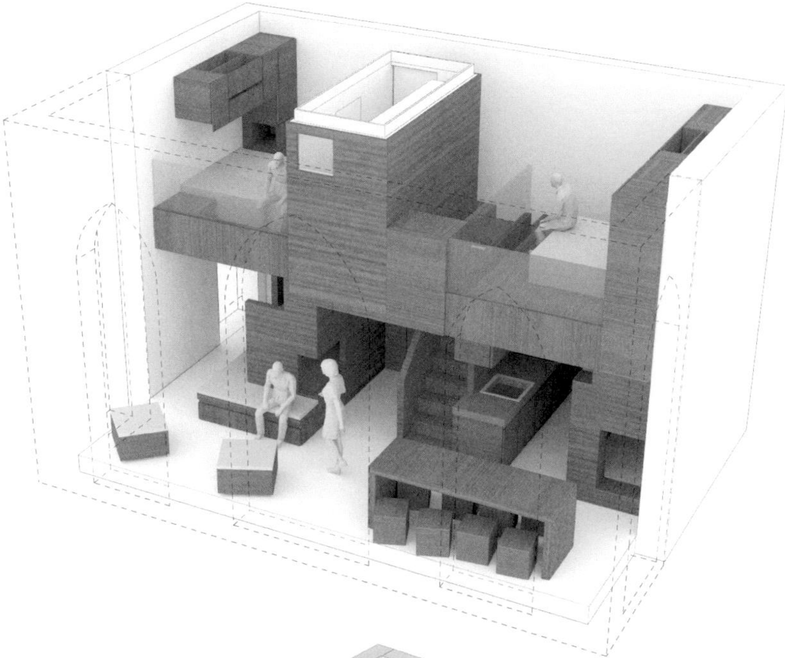

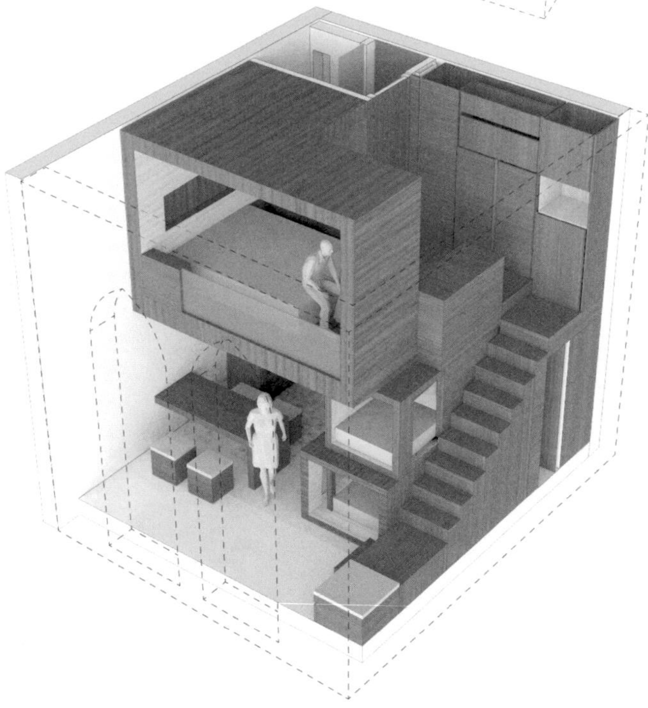

The idea was to create a pedestrian square on Place de la Madeleine linked to the church and relating to its surroundings. The square offers a large surface area that can be appropriated by passers-by as well as bicycle paths with new, protected crossings. To create the furniture, we relied on an object that has become iconic, identity-related and, paradoxically, almost banal: the bench designed by the architect Gabriel Davioud during the Second Empire, more than 100,000 of which have since been installed in public spaces in Paris. Its constructional system is simple: wooden slats supported by cast iron uprights fixed to the ground, with seats facing in one or both directions. It seemed obvious to us that stretching the bench would better emphasise the ambient space and provide a closer match with the scale of the square. The bench curves naturally to create a place, wraps itself around a tree to anchor itself in its context, extends to become a table, just as the numerous other features of the square offer uses of their own. Together with the play of curves and counter-curves, the bench's variable size demarcates a range of seating and any number of sitting positions.

Il s'agissait de créer sur la place de la Madeleine un parvis piétonnier en lien avec l'église et connecté aux éléments qui la bordent. Ce parvis offre une vaste surface appropriable par les passants ainsi que des cheminements cyclables qui permettent de nouvelles traversées protégées. Pour créer le mobilier, nous nous sommes appuyés sur un objet devenu iconique, identitaire et, paradoxalement, presque banal : le banc dessiné par l'architecte Gabriel Davioud sous le Second Empire, déployé à plus de 100 000 exemplaires dans l'espace public parisien. Son système constructif est simple : des lames de bois fixées sur un piétement en fonte scellé au sol. Le banc se décline en assises simples ou à double orientation. Il nous a semblé évident de l'étirer afin de mieux souligner l'espace et de le mettre à l'échelle de la place. Le banc se courbe naturellement pour créer un lieu, vient s'enrouler autour d'un arbre pour s'ancrer dans son contexte, se prolonge pour devenir table. Les implantations multiples sur la place offrent un panel de situations qui génèrent autant d'usages. L'ampleur plus ou moins importante de l'objet comme le jeu des courbes et contre-courbes définissent une gamme d'assises diversifiées qui ouvrent à une infinité de postures.

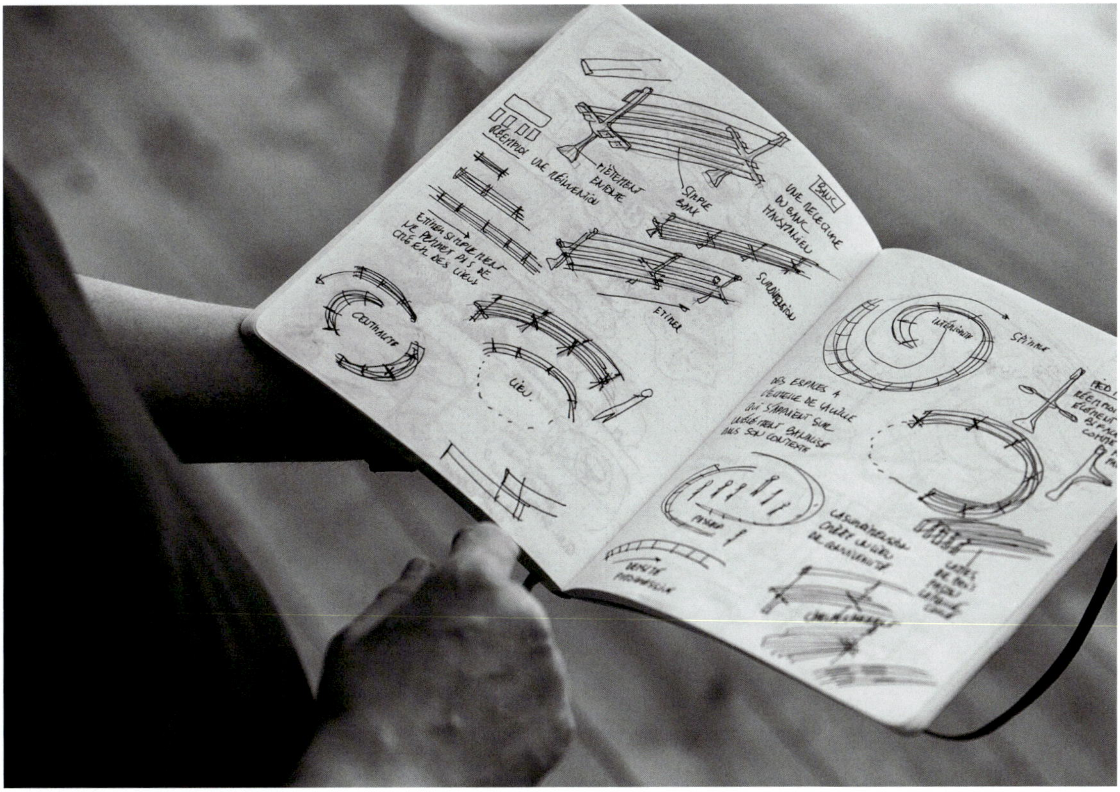

Place de la Madeleine, Paris

Place de la Madeleine, Paris

Place de la Madeleine, Paris

Place de la Madeleine, Paris

"Sometimes evaluating the degree of transformation of a site initially involves deprogramming. Then comes a reprogramming based on the site's uses and meaning. None of the ideas put forward receive immediate recognition. Our projects develop gradually out of variations."

« Évaluer le niveau de transformation d’un site, c’est parfois procéder d’abord à sa dé-programmation. La reprogrammation s’appuie ensuite sur les usages et le sens des lieux. De toutes les hypothèses émises, aucune ne s’impose immédiatement. Nos projets émergent graduellement, par variations. »

Facing the Seine and part of an ensemble built for the World's Fair in 1937, the Paris Museum of Modern Art ensures the topographical transition between Avenue du Président-Wilson at the top of the plot and the embankment at the bottom. The aim of the redevelopment project was to improve reception facilities for the public and working conditions for the personnel. With plenty of room for potential appropriations, the space has been redesigned as a flexible, manageable, event-friendly venue. With an eye to the site's monumental pre-War architecture, our project parleyed with matters of grand scale and original geometry. The 1937 building, its modernity tempered with a classical vocabulary, is made of concrete faced with stone, which confers thickness. Our project played on these interstitial spaces, using them to accommodate service and technical facilities and thus avoiding encroachment on the big interior volumes. We've reconnected with the city, doing away with some of the alterations that ensued between the actual construction and our intervention. The transformation is visible from the forecourt and the entrance. The windows, covered up by the previous changes to the interior, have regained their crucial role of catching the visitor's eye and directing it towards the view of Paris, in a generous osmosis between interior and exterior.

Face à la Seine, le musée d'Art moderne de Paris fait partie d'un ensemble construit pour l'Exposition universelle de 1937 ; il assure une transition topographique entre l'avenue du Président-Wilson, en haut de la parcelle, et le quai, en contrebas. Son réaménagement avait pour objet de renouveler les conditions d'accueil du public comme celles de travail du personnel. Tout en ménageant une large place aux potentielles appropriations futures, l'espace est mis en forme pour susciter l'événement, offrant un lieu permissif et maniable. Afin de composer avec l'architecture monumentale d'avant guerre, notre projet dialogue avec la grande échelle et sa géométrie originelle. Le bâtiment de 1937, d'une modernité tempérée par un vocabulaire classique, est fait de béton doublé d'un parement de pierre, ce qui lui confère une épaisseur. Notre projet exploite ces entre-deux-parois pour y loger les services et éléments techniques, ce qui a permis de ne pas empiéter sur les grands volumes des espaces intérieurs. Nous avons retissé le lien à la ville, vers laquelle le musée s'ouvre à nouveau, effaçant certains remaniements réalisés entre la construction originelle et notre intervention. La refonte du bâtiment est visible dès l'entrée, à l'échelle du parvis. Les ouvertures, masquées par les précédents aménagements intérieurs, retrouvent le rôle prépondérant qu'elles avaient initialement ; elles orientent le regard du visiteur, qui se dirige naturellement vers elles pour contempler la vue sur Paris, offrant une large perméabilité entre intérieur et extérieur.

Les collections du musée
Salle Matisse
Librairie
BOOKSHOP
Les Amis du musée
Sortie

Information

Accueil
groupes
Visites guidées
Activités

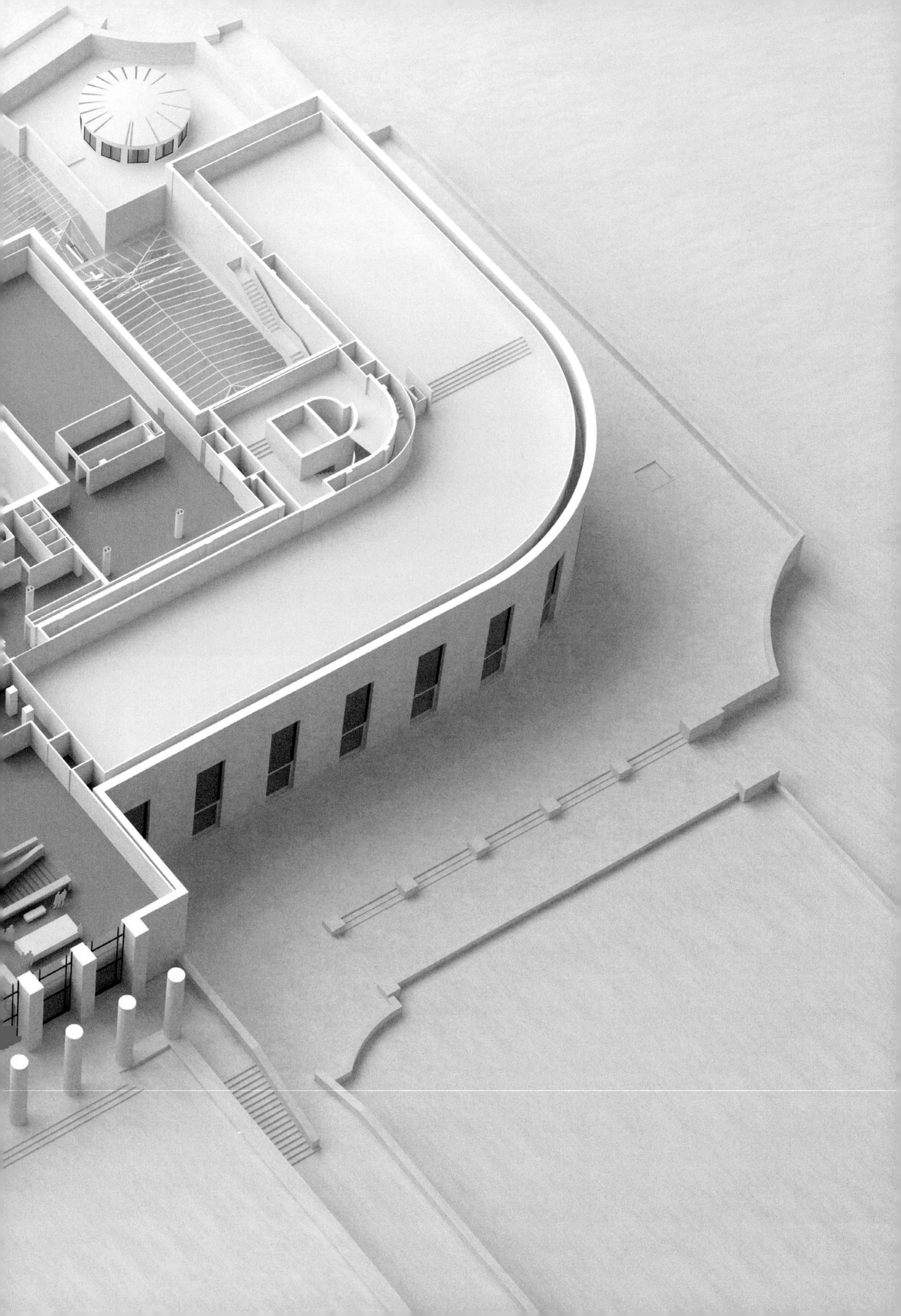

SORTIE
DE
SECOURS

Fly

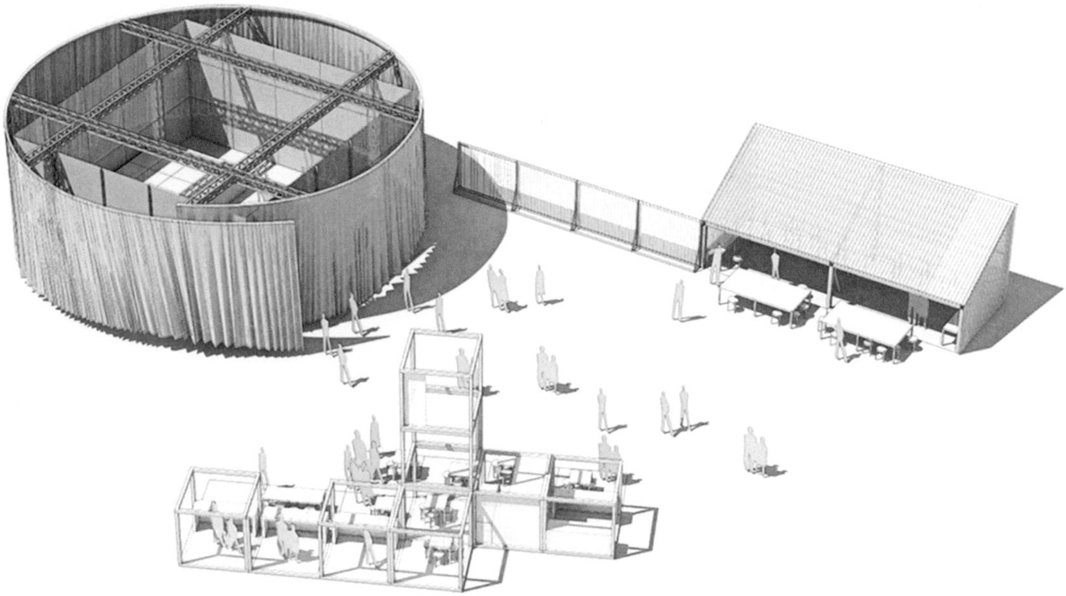

Micro-Folie

Based on the specifications drawn up by Bernard Tschumi, this Micro-Folie was designed as a reproducible prototype, an experience of mobile, ephemeral architecture that would transpose the intensity of Paris's Parc de la Villette version to other sites and abroad. Modules for different uses were developed: the first, comprising a cafe, library and toy library, was a place of welcome and sharing; the second, a workshop and fablab, was an opportunity for inventing and making; and the last, equipped with an immersive digital museum and a stage, encouraged discovery and spreading your wings. Each space was conceived as a unique scenographic entity with its own logic. Systems and layouts were adapted to the venue concerned. Thus in all sorts of ways the resultant public space generated different situations and set up physical and visual connections between a variety of audiences. The architectural side was created out of elements that come together, resist or disappear. What we sought to bring about in this project is an event whose possibilities must appear spontaneous and infinite, and whose architecture must be imbued with a capacity for transformation.

Cette micro-folie, prototype conçu pour être reproductible, a été imaginée en fonction du cahier des charges élaboré par Bernard Tschumi. Cette expérience d'architecture mobile et éphémère transpose l'intensité du parc de la Villette dans d'autres lieux, y compris à l'étranger. Des modules aux usages différenciés ont été développés : le premier, qui se décline en café, bibliothèque et ludothèque, permet d'accueillir et de partager. Le second, aménagé en atelier et en fablab, propose d'inventer et de fabriquer ; le dernier, pourvu d'un musée numérique immersif et d'une scène, incite à découvrir et à rayonner. Chaque espace est pensé comme un dispositif scénographique unique, avec sa logique propre. Dispositifs et agencements s'ajustent en fonction du lieu qui les accueille. L'espace public ainsi créé génère des situations variées, établit des liens physiques et visuels entre des publics divers, selon des usages multiples. L'architecture est produite par les éléments qui s'assemblent, résistent ou disparaissent. Ce que nous avons cherché à susciter dans ce projet, c'est l'événement : les possibilités doivent apparaître spontanées et infinies, l'architecture doit porter une capacité de transformation.

"When our projects reach the point of being too intricate, we have to simplify in the interests of appropriateness and clarity. We do our best to cultivate generosity and not slide into desiccation, just as we do everything possible to ensure the right accidents. Combining knowledge with know-how and purpose, and with experiment and intuition, allows us to compose and associate rather than impose and enforce."

« Quand nos projets atteignent un niveau d'intrication trop important, il nous faut les simplifier pour accéder à une forme de justesse, d'évidence. Nous nous efforçons de cultiver la générosité, de ne pas glisser dans l'assèchement. Toutes les dispositions sont prises pour que les bons accidents arrivent. Conjuguer connaissances, savoir-faire et intentions avec empirisme, expérimentations et intuitions permet de composer et d'associer plutôt que d'imposer et de soumettre. »

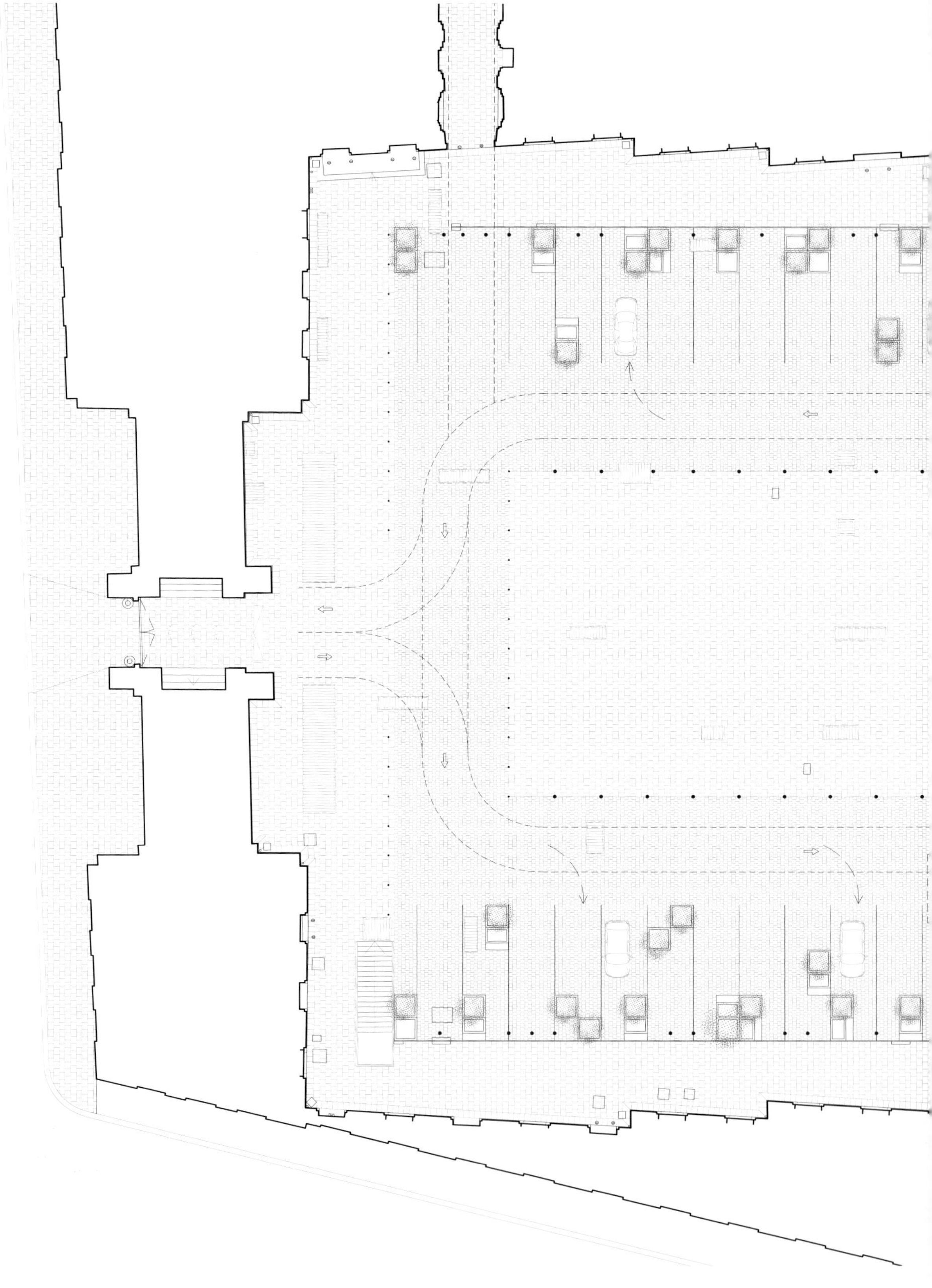

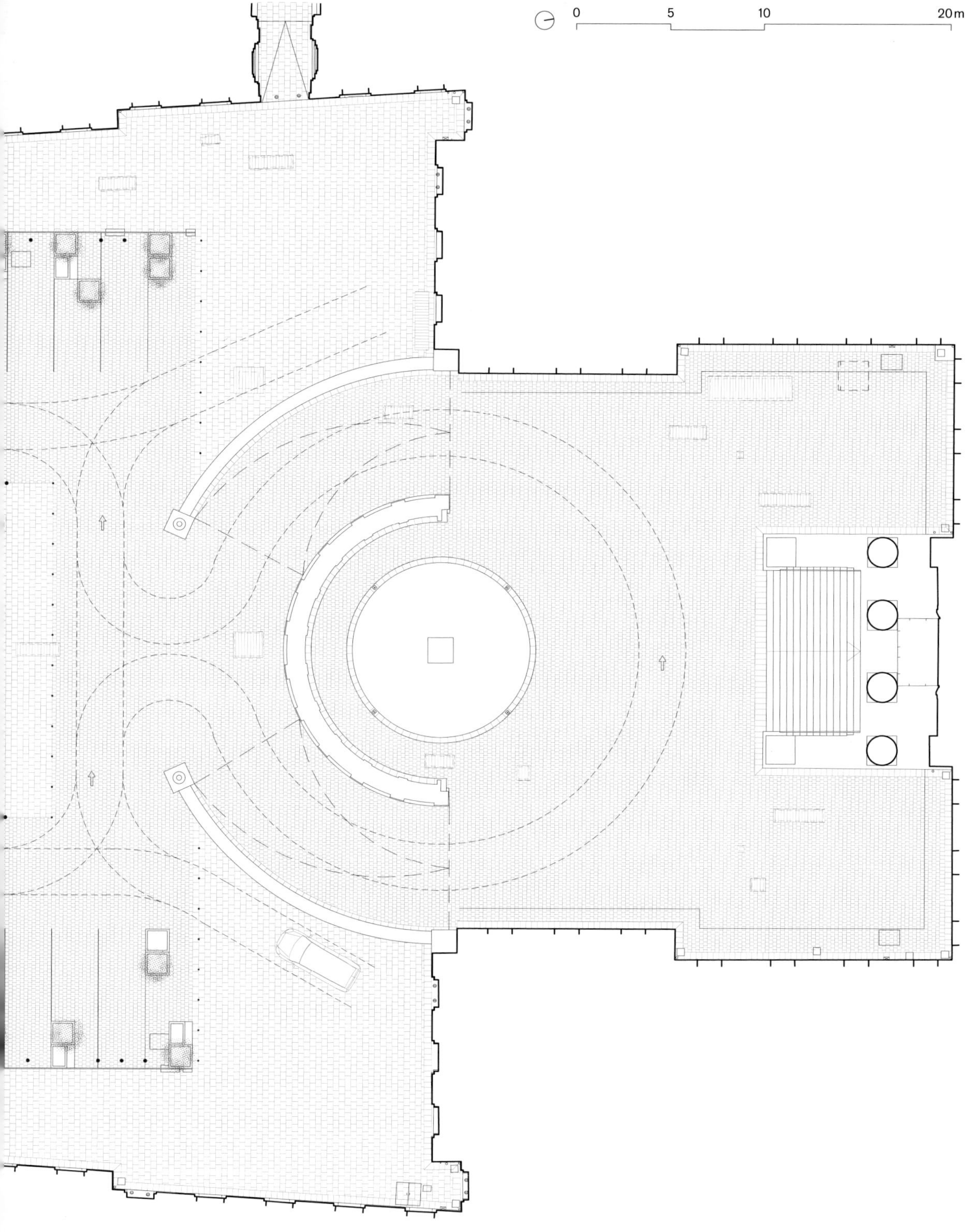
0
5
10
20 m

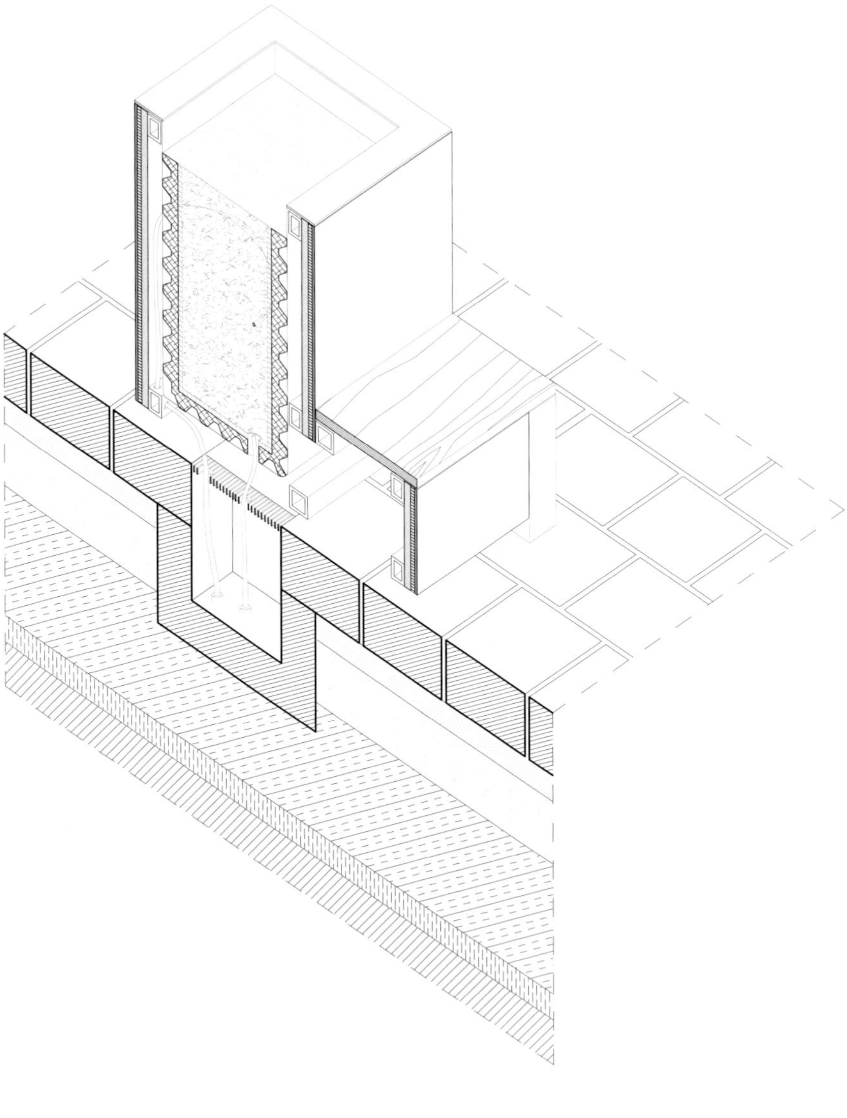

The aim here was to enhance the public embodiment of parliamentary representation while accommodating everyday uses, and to bridge the gap between the scale of the human body and the symbolic scale of the site's monumental character. What seems to be a courtyard is actually the roof of a five-storey underground building, home to a maze of offices and galleries. The technical complexity this involves has been masked by maximising the integration of the constraints into the narrow space between the slab of the subterranean building and the surface of the courtyard, and thus preserving the clarity and legibility of the layout. User itineraries are numerous and of variable density. The planters dotted around the courtyard are connected to an automatic sprinkler system and can be moved about, creating protected configurations to be appropriated at will.

Il s'agissait ici de mettre en valeur l'espace public de la représentation parlementaire tout en accueillant des usages quotidiens, de faire le grand écart entre l'échelle du corps humain et celle, symbolique, de la monumentalité du lieu. L'espace perçu comme une cour est en réalité le toit d'un bâtiment enterré de cinq étages, truffé d'émergences et de galeries. La complexité technique de ces dispositifs a été masquée en intégrant au maximum les contraintes dans la faible épaisseur disponible entre la dalle du bâtiment enterré et le sol de la cour afin de conserver à l'aménagement sa clarté et sa lisibilité. Les cheminements des usagers sont multiples, leur densité varie. Les bacs plantés qui ponctuent l'espace, raccordés à un système d'arrosage automatique, sont déplaçables : chacun d'eux intègre des assises, créant autant d'espaces protégés laissés à l'appropriation de tout un chacun.

Sitting in the monumental courtyard, he props his trainers on the bench and stretches his back muscles. In very high heels, she hunches over her phone. He's sitting upright in his suit on the last few inches of the plank. She tilts her head back, making the most of late winter's first sharp rays of sunlight. Curves, angles, folds, concrete, wood, steel: inhabited urban furniture creates transitory places for pursuits engaging the body, space and function. Small scale inspires large. It probes habits, gauges aesthetic resistance like that of materials. The furniture is a direct testing of the body. What does sitting down mean? And waiting? Are postures different in a waiting room and a public place? Shape has no time for the arbitrary; it has to react immediately to whoever uses it. **FL**

Assis dans la cour monumentale, il pose ses baskets sur le banc et étire son dos. Longs talons aiguilles, elle se penche dans sa conversation téléphonique. Lui est droit dans son costume, assis sur les dix derniers centimètres de la planche. Celui-là repose sa tête, profite des premiers rayons de soleil crus de la sortie de l'hiver. Courbes, angles, plis, béton, bois, acier, les mobiliers habités créent des lieux transitoires de recherche qui engagent le corps, l'espace et la fonction. La petite échelle informe la grande. Elle teste des habitudes, évalue les résistances esthétiques comme celle des matériaux. Le mobilier est une épreuve directe avec le corps. Qu'est-ce que s'asseoir ? Qu'est-ce qu'attendre ? Les postures sont-elles différentes dans une salle d'attente et dans un lieu public ? La forme ne souffre pas l'arbitraire, elle doit répondre séance tenante à celui qui s'en sert. **FL**

 Reception of the French National Assembly, Paris

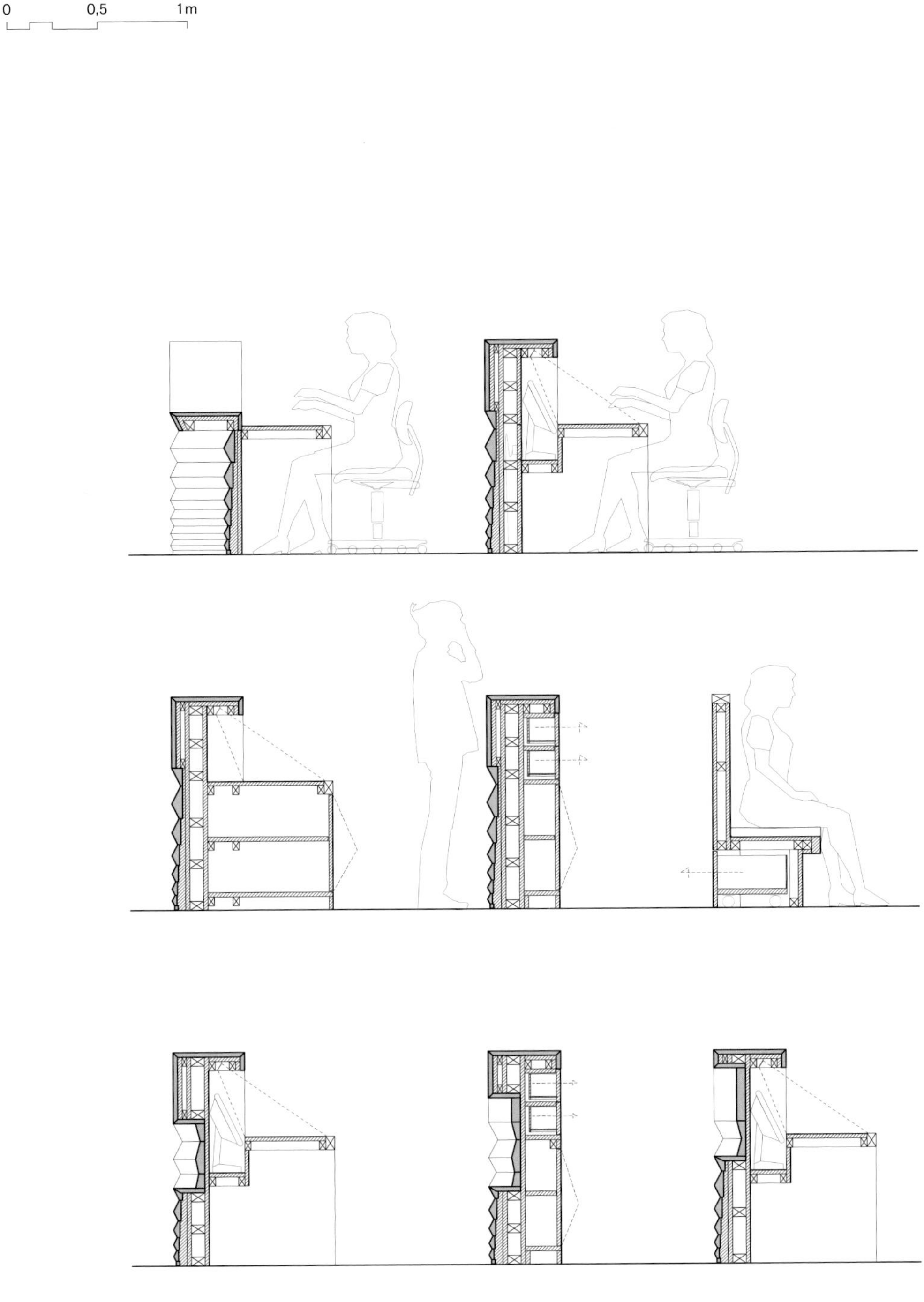
0
0,5
1m

The architecture of the National Assembly must concretely represent the institution's programmatic and symbolic reception functions. The image of parliamentary transparency guided our project, organising both its perception and the fluidity of its traffic flows. Technical and security complexities were concealed, while the precision and user-friendliness of each feature had to be evident: thus the bulletproof glass seems to have been chosen solely for its transparent quality and the solid oak of the work stations for a certain monumental feel. The ribbed Givet bluestone underscores the role of the reception desk as the project's focal point.

L'architecture de l'Assemblée nationale se doit de représenter concrètement les fonctions programmatiques et symboliques d'accueil de cette institution. L'image de la transparence parlementaire a guidé notre projet, organisé sa perception comme la fluidité de ses parcours. Les complexités techniques et sécuritaires ont été dissimulées. La précision et l'ergonomie de chaque élément devaient être évidentes. Ainsi le verre pare-balles semble-t-il employé uniquement pour ses qualités de transparence et les postes des agents, en chêne massif, dégagent-ils une certaine monumentalité. La pierre bleue de Givet se plisse pour former le comptoir d'accueil de l'Assemblée, point névralgique de l'aménagement.

 La Cabotte reception pavilion, Mondragon

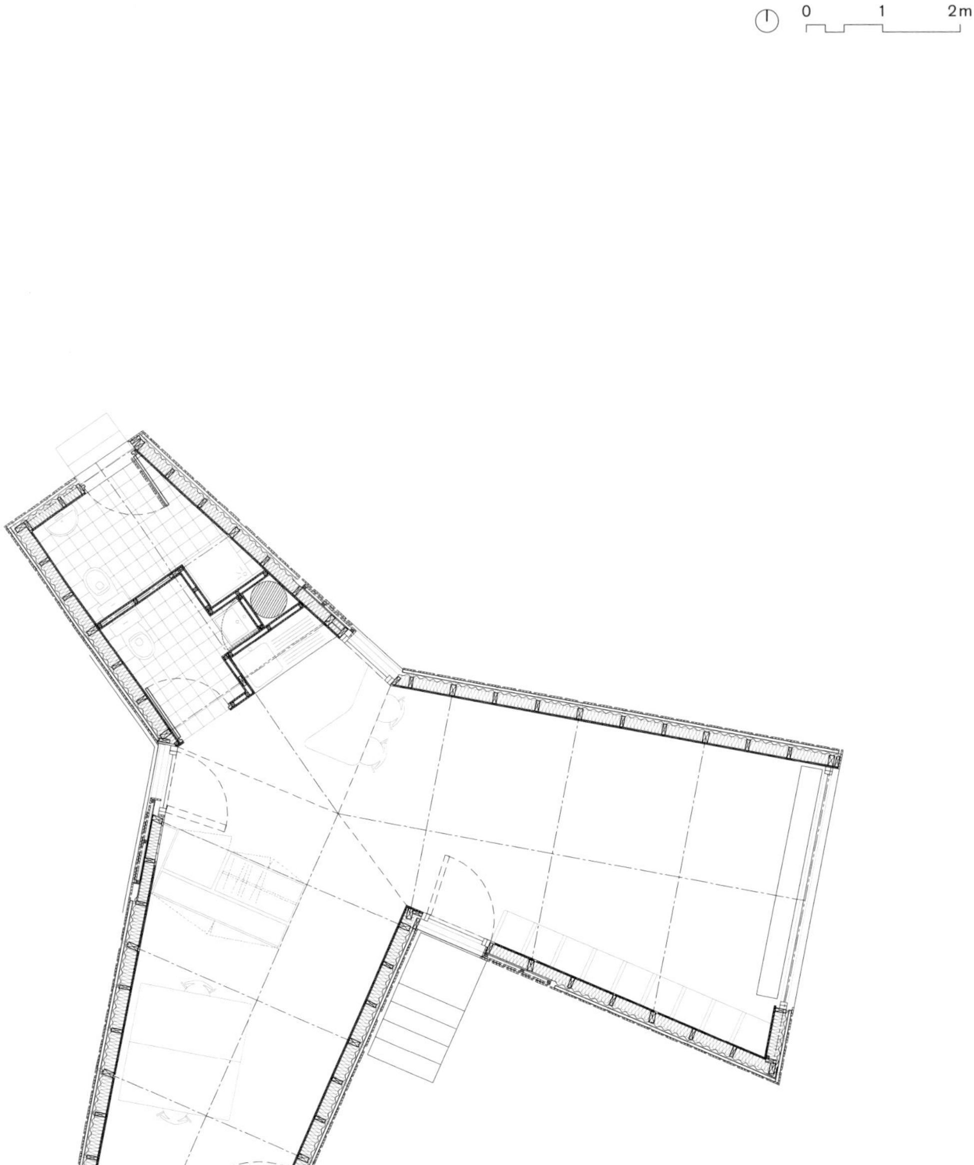
0
1
2 m

La Cabotte reception pavilion, Mondragon

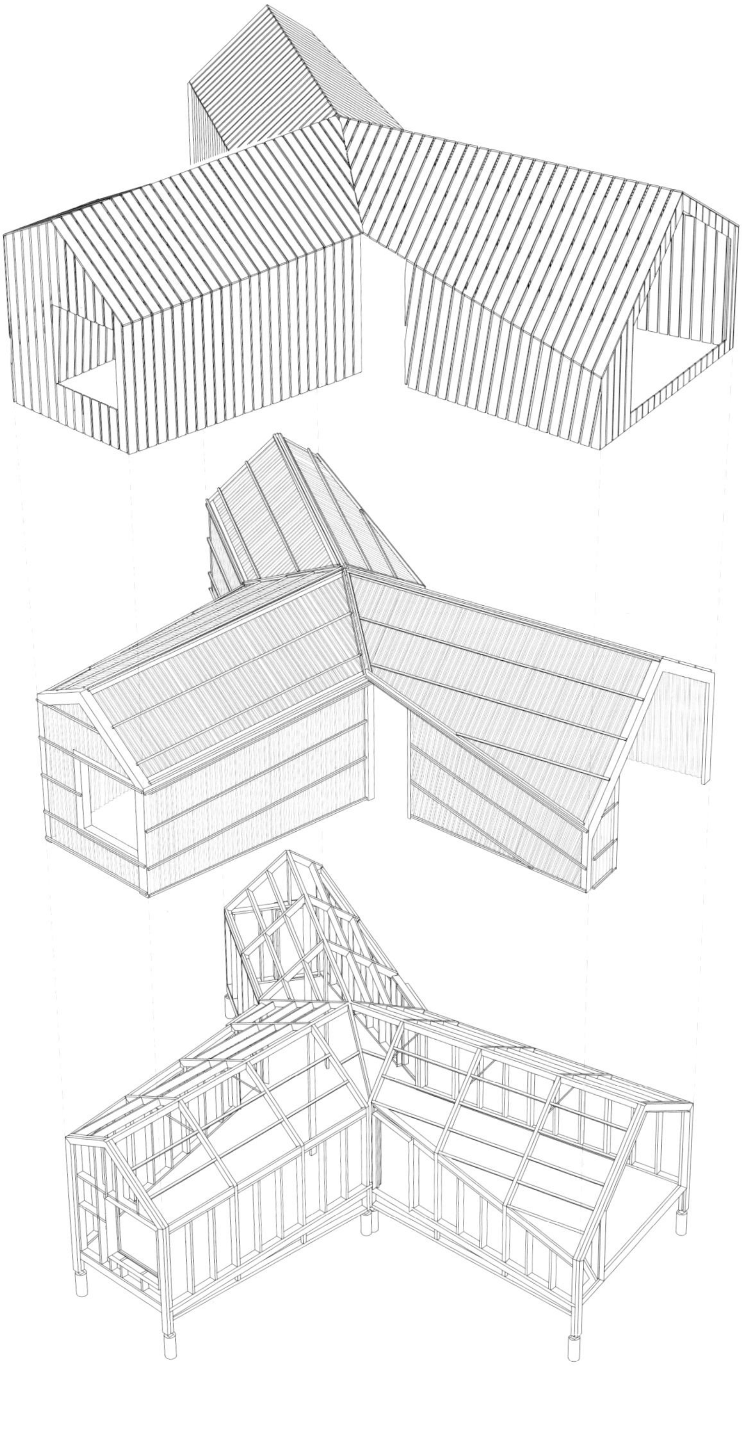

Our clients' attachment to their winery was a major influence on the architecture of this reception pavilion, and in particular on its roots in the local. The three-part construction suggests a compact piece of furniture sitting on the slope, a domestic inhabitant of the wide open spaces. We gave it feet to let it settle in gently, as if free to move about or slip away. Each of the three segments hosts a specific programme and framing of the landscape: the entrance to the estate is visible from the offices, the utilities are set against the hillside, the reception/tasting area opens out generously onto the vineyards – all this against the backdrop of Mount Ventoux. The materiality of the wooden envelope takes a back seat: once patinated, it blends perfectly into the landscape, and only the straight-line geometry of the assembled boards remains.

L'attachement de nos clients à leur domaine viticole a fortement influencé l'architecture de ce pavillon d'accueil, notamment son accroche au territoire. La construction, tripartite, évoque un meuble compact posé sur le coteau, tel un mobilier domestique habitant le grand paysage. Nous lui avons donné des pieds pour qu'il s'installe délicatement, comme s'il pouvait se déplacer ou s'effacer. Chacune des trois branches accueille un programme spécifique tout en cadrant le paysage : l'entrée du domaine est visible des bureaux, les services s'adossent au coteau, l'accueil-espace de dégustation s'ouvre généreusement vers les vignes avec, en fond de scène, le mont Ventoux. La matérialité de l'enveloppe en bois passe au second plan : une fois patinée, elle s'intègre parfaitement dans le paysage, seules restent les lignes géométriques créées par l'assemblage des planches.

The volumes of these three pavilions curve, stretch or pleat according to their use. Devoted respectively to reception, catering and visitor services, they are situated on a strip of parkland running along the banks of the Seine.
The orchestration and density of the planted thoroughfare interconnect the buildings, which make light of a complex setting as they glide around trees and beneath their foliage, and offer generous views of the scenery. Their envelope of wooden and stainless steel slats sets up interaction with the ambient vegetation amid a proliferation of reflections and points of view.

Les volumes de ces trois pavillons se courbent, se tendent ou se plissent au gré de leurs usages. Dédiés respectivement à l'accueil, à la restauration et au service, ils s'inscrivent dans un parc linéaire en bord de Seine. Le rythme et la densité du mail planté font le lien entre les constructions, qui s'enroulent autour des arbres et se glissent sous leurs frondaisons, contournant naturellement leur complexité. Les pavillons sont largement ouverts sur le paysage. Leur enveloppe en lames de bois et acier inox crée un dialogue avec la végétation environnante, démultipliant reflets et perspectives.

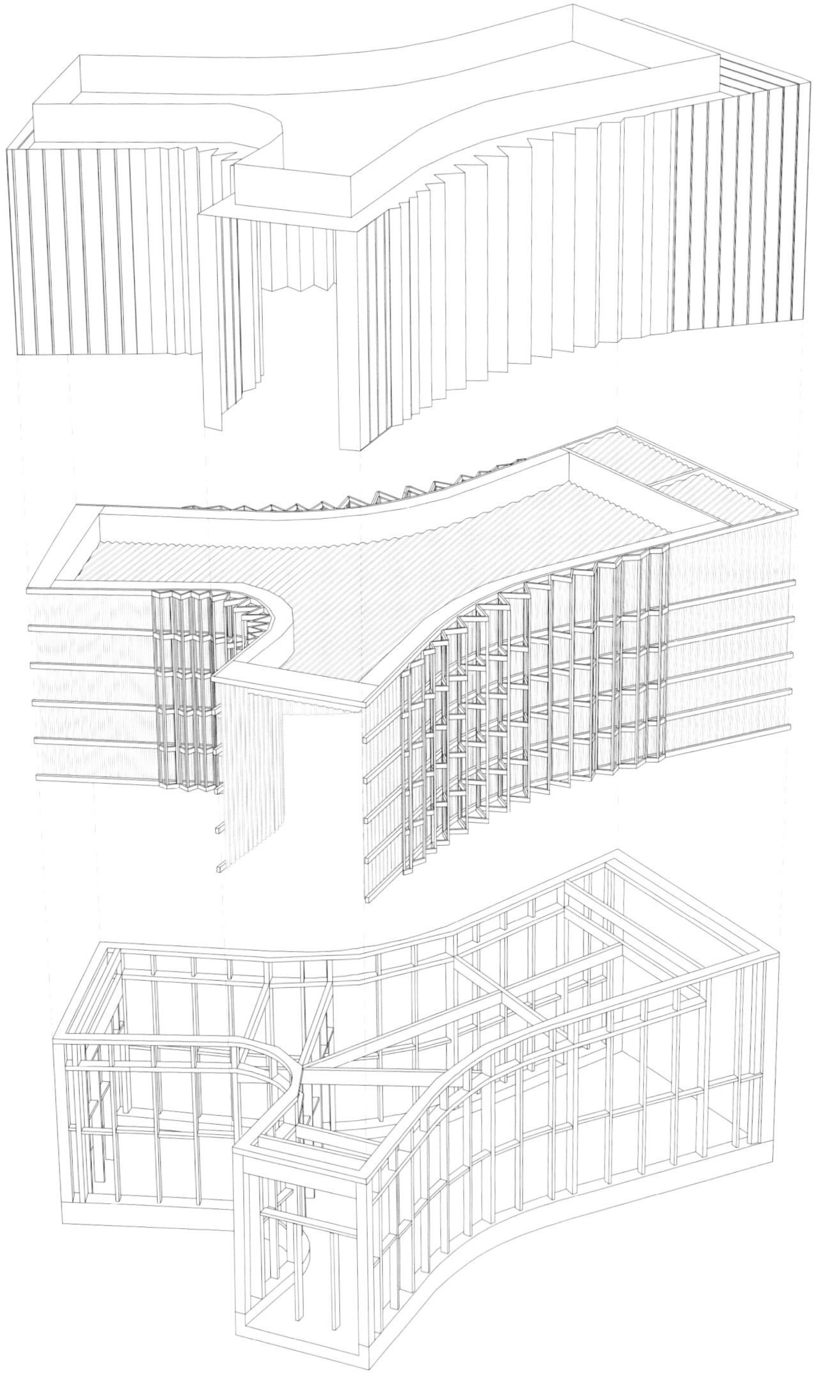

"Leaving a project open-ended is an elementary form of politeness. Dwelling is space's capacity to welcome acts of generosity and attentiveness. By keeping ample scope for future appropriation, our projects open up perspectives of welcome and trigger events. Planning ahead means never trying to deal with all the issues at once. We constantly adapt to the situation, the building process and the economics."

« Laisser un projet ouvert est une forme de politesse élémentaire. L'habiter, c'est la capacité de l'espace à accueillir générosités et attentions. En ménageant une large place pour l'appropriation future, nos projets ouvrent des possibilités d'accueil et suscitent des événements. Projeter, c'est ne jamais chercher à tout résoudre d'un seul coup. Nous nous adaptons sans cesse à la situation, au chantier, à l'économie. »

One side. Fixing our bikes to the metal bar with the same padlock. Sitting on the steps, whispering the latest news then squeezing up, legs touching, because someone wants to get through. You blush. Boiling hot coffee, eyes closed, just behind the window with its pale ray of winter sunlight. Presentation. Hands moist in the dark, screening. No one speaks, I'm trembling. *Ping* of a distant microwave. A young woman steps out of her office, the straps of her dress graphically echoed by the light-streaked pedestrian flow. I have to concentrate. The other side. He's just run the mop over the orange and is sure to take a break before moving on to the grey, like every other night. The lights betray the dust. The night watchman has a cold. Chairs upended on the tables, mop questing for crumbs. Sixth microwave cleaned. Hey, a mainframe's been left on. A little blinking light, a firefly lost in the deserted building. **FL**

Endroit. Attacher nos vélos ensemble, sur la barre, avec le même cadenas. S'asseoir sur les marches, chuchoter les dernières nouvelles et puis se serrer, jambe contre jambe, parce que quelqu'un veut passer. Tu rougis. Café brûlant, yeux fermés, juste derrière la fenêtre où perce un pâle rayon de soleil d'hiver. Présentation. Les mains moites dans le noir, projection. Personne ne parle, je tremble. « Ting » du micro-onde au loin. Une jeune femme quitte son bureau dans la circulation zébrée de lumière, pendant graphique des bretelles de sa robe. Je dois me concentrer. Envers. Il finit de passer la serpillière sur le orange et fera certainement une pause avant de passer au gris, comme chaque nuit. Les luminaires dénoncent la poussière. Le veilleur de nuit est enrhumé. Chaises retournées sur les tables, serpillière en quête de miettes. Sixième micro-onde nettoyé. Tiens, une unité centrale est restée allumée. Loupiote qui clignote, luciole perdue dans l'architecture désertée. **FL**

Pépinière d'entreprises, Bourg-lès-Valence

Conversion of this former industrial site brought transformation of three market halls into new workplaces, including a digital animation centre and studios dedicated to computer graphics. The whole system had to remain flexible and scalable. Once the envelope was renovated, each segment found its specific character. Three parallel naves, adjacent and sliding elegantly together. Lit by a sawtooth roof, the central hall houses the common areas – refectory, café, kitchen. Colour here and there creates more intimate spaces, on a domestic scale; the coloured surfaces – walls or floors – suffice to highlight and shape specific "spots" with recourse to very limited means. The second hall is a unitary, open-plan workspace overlooked by a mezzanine, an independent element that adds further possible uses. The third hall is divided up into compartments for more private ventures.

La reconversion de cet ancien site industriel a permis de transformer trois halles en nouveaux lieux de travail, parmi lesquels un pôle d'animation numérique et des studios dédiés à la création infographique. L'ensemble devait rester flexible et évolutif. Une fois l'enveloppe rénovée, chaque nef a trouvé sa spécificité. Trois vaisseaux parallèles se jouxtent et coulissent entre eux. La halle centrale, éclairée par des sheds, accueille les espaces communs – réfectoire, café, cuisine. L'emploi ponctuel de la couleur y crée des espaces plus intimes, à l'échelle domestique ; les surfaces colorées – murs ou sols – suffisent à souligner et à mettre en forme des « lieux » spécifiques, dans une grande économie de moyens. La seconde nef, conservée ouverte, forme un espace de travail unitaire surmonté d'une mezzanine, élément autonome qui multiplie les possibilités d'occupation. La troisième, compartimentée, accueille des ateliers de travail plus confidentiels.

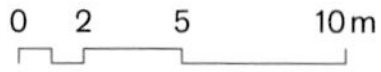
0 2 5 10 m

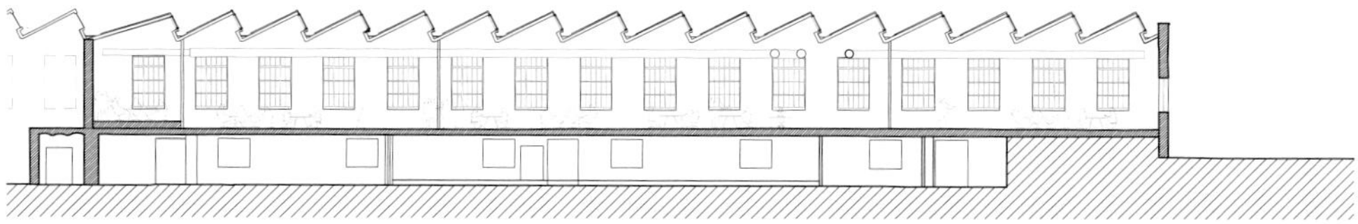

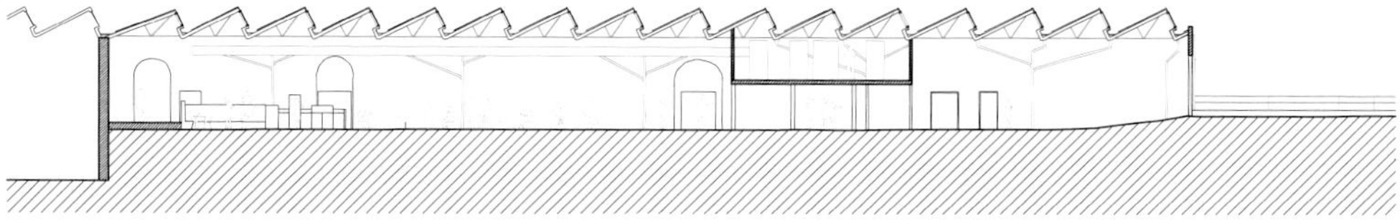

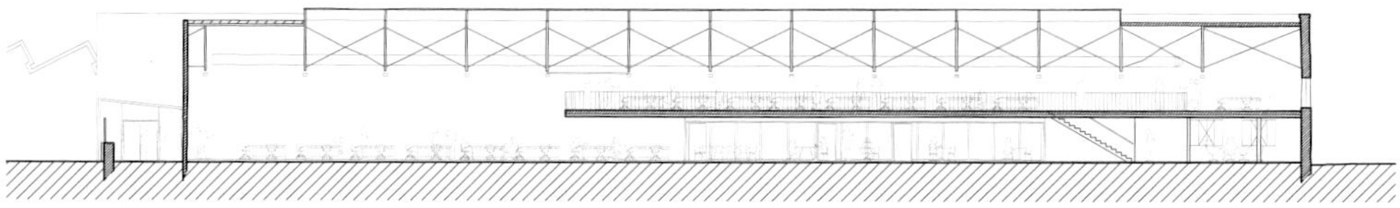

LAVAZZA

Pépinière d'entreprises, Bourg-lès-Valence

The new archivists' workspaces at the National Audiovisual Institute (INA) are housed in a building dating from 1972, a typical example of the French precast concrete system, with its much-appreciated capacity for reconfiguration. Unfortunately the modular structure had lost in legibility over the years. Our project drew on the regularity of its constructional grid and the atmosphere thus generated. Decompartmentalised and stripped down, the space regained its unity, with the grid then serving as the matrix for new separation methods and for furniture adapted to the scale of the human body. The project was also an opportunity to adapt the volumes to contemporary professional practice. The dimensions were carefully adjusted to ensure a dedicated space for all, while transparent partitions between workspaces favoured porosity and new synergies. Matching the scale of the building, the raw materiality of concrete found its counterpart in the mellowness of wooden furniture matching the scale of the user.

Les nouveaux espaces de travail des documentalistes de l'Institut national de l'audiovisuel (INA) prennent place dans un bâtiment datant de 1972, caractéristique de la préfabrication en béton française. Sa qualité réside dans sa capacité de reconfiguration. Mais au fil du temps, sa structure modulaire avait perdu de sa lisibilité. Notre projet s'appuie sur le rythme régulier de la trame constructive et l'atmosphère qu'elle génère. L'espace, décloisonné, a été mis à nu pour retrouver son unité. La trame sert de matrice aux nouveaux éléments de séparation et au mobilier, qui s'ajuste à l'échelle du corps. Le projet a également été l'occasion d'adapter les volumes aux usages professionnels contemporains. Les dimensions sont réglées avec attention pour que chacun puisse disposer d'un espace dédié. La transparence des cloisonnements conserve une porosité entre les espaces, favorisant de nouvelles synergies. La matérialité brute du béton, à l'échelle du bâtiment, trouve son pendant dans la douceur du mobilier en bois, à l'échelle de l'usager.

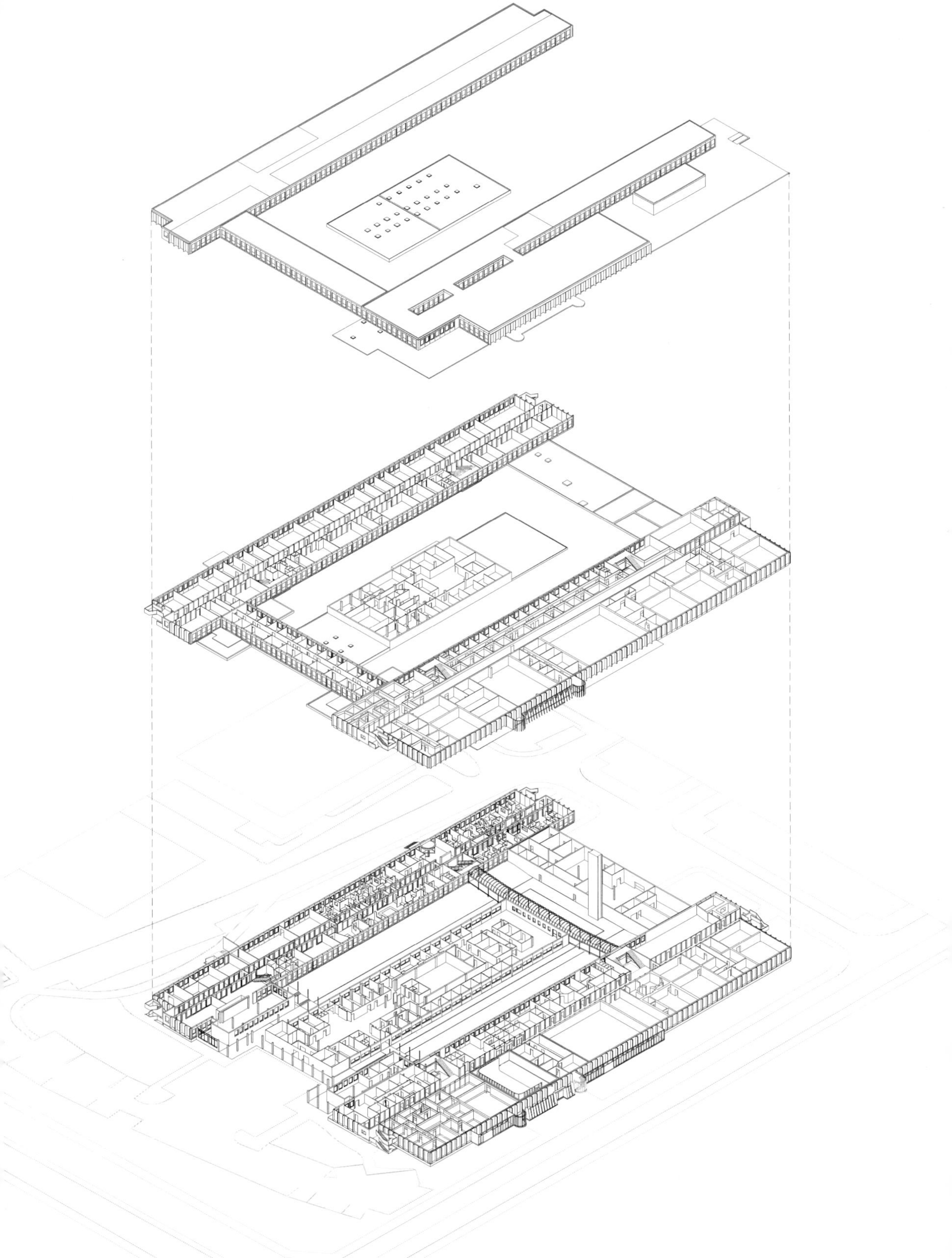

Studios
Production

Studios
Production

Prefabricated structures, 1975. Slip inside and fill with wood. Cold and warm, industrial and domestic, mineral and vegetal. A ceiling of mineral sprayed concrete, exposed beams and chases. The work around the joinery reads as cutting, fixing and fresh cement jointing. The corridor ducts emerge on either side of the suspended ceiling. From grainy to smooth: an urge to touch the building, rub up against the architecture, piques the office workers back after the renovations. The new workspace separation modules are home to the hundreds of wires needed to feed dual screens, keyboards, mainframes, electric jugs, speakers, casual lighting, fans, printers and telephones. The fine, fragile trajectory of bamboo begonia stalks. Slender, tufted *beaucarnea*. Wandering Jew with its leaves drooping towards the floor. *Zamioculcas* branches in their upward assault. Everyone working with headphones clamped on like foliate excrescences, protective veneers. Silence. Light. Concentration. **FL**

Portiques préfabriqués, 1975. S'y glisser, remplir de bois. Froid et chaud, industriel et domestique, minéral et végétal.
Au plafond, béton floqué en sous-face, poutres brutes, saignées. Autour des menuiseries, les interventions se lisent : découpe, installation, colmatage en ciment frais. Les gaines du couloir se dévoilent de part et d'autre du plafond technique. Du granuleux au lisse, une envie de toucher le bâtiment, de se frotter à l'architecture agite les salariés venus reprendre possession de leur bureau après les travaux. Les modules de séparation des nouveaux espaces de travail nichent les centaines de fils nécessaires pour nourrir doubles écrans, claviers, unités centrales, bouilloires, enceintes, lampes d'appoint, ventilateurs, imprimantes ou téléphones. Trajectoire fine et fragile des tiges de deux bégonias bambous. Graciles touffes d'un *beaucarnea*. Une misère étire ses feuilles vers le sol. Les branches du *zamioculcas* se lancent dans un assaut aérien. Chacun travaille le casque sur les oreilles, comme deux excroissances lobées, feuilles de protection. Silence. Lumière. Concentration. **FL**

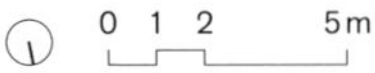
0 1 2 5m

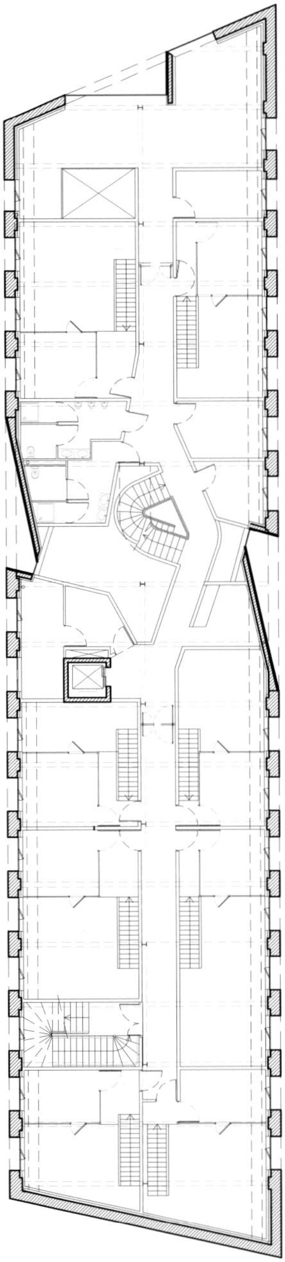

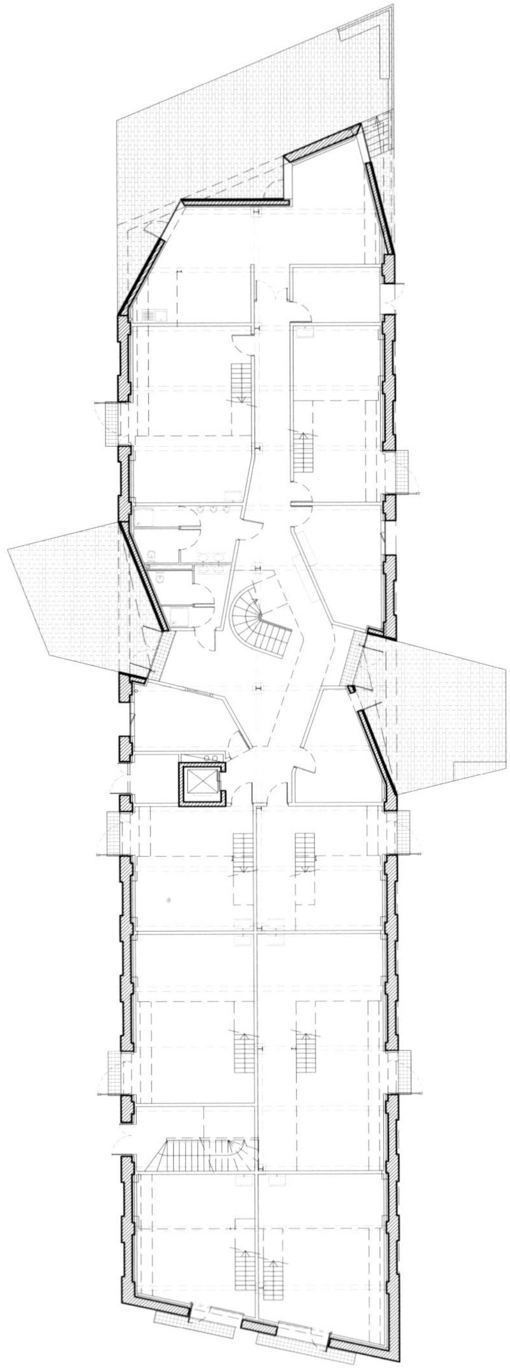

The old packaging factory in the heart of Pont-Audemer remained a wounding sign of the town's industrial collapse. Now, rehabilitated and transformed into a business incubator, it has become an urban signal, the first stone in a patient rebuilding process. Reprogramming has brought the brownfield site back to life, and the offices and workshops of the business incubator are now complemented by a training centre. Our aim was to make the most of the useful space while sticking to a credo of simplicity served by limited resources. We wanted to make things happen, trigger interplay and exchanges and synergies with a view to attracting businesses and helping them develop. The central circulation core and its ramifications dilate, stretch, perforate the facades and create connections on an urban as well as an architectural scale. Openings and views link the building to its landscape and the river Risle flowing by just below. Adapting to user practice, LED-lit footways widen in places into squares or interior streets. The metamorphosis has done its work: barely completed, the incubator is already facing overload.

Au cœur de Pont-Audemer, l'ancienne cartonnerie demeurait le signe blessant de la faillite industrielle de la ville. Réhabilitée et transformée en pépinière d'entreprises, elle est devenue signal urbain, première pierre d'une patiente reconstruction. La friche vit à nouveau grâce à sa reprogrammation. Aux bureaux et ateliers de la pépinière s'ajoute un centre de formation. Notre intervention avait pour objectif de mettre en valeur l'espace utile, tout en suivant un principe de simplicité et d'économie de moyens. Il s'agissait, pour nous, de faire événement, de provoquer croisements, échanges et synergies, en vue d'accueillir des entreprises, et d'aider à leur développement. Le noyau de circulation central et ses ramifications se dilatent, s'étirent, perforent les façades pour tisser des liens, à l'échelle architecturale mais aussi urbaine. Ouvertures et cadrages mettent en lien le bâtiment avec le paysage et la Risle, qui coule à ses pieds. Les cheminements, soulignés par la lumière, s'élargissent par endroits en places ou en rues intérieures, s'adaptant aux pratiques des usagers. Le lieu, métamorphosé, attire de nombreux candidats : à peine achevée, la pépinière est déjà trop petite.

LA CARTONNERIE
PEPINIERE
D'ENTREPRISES

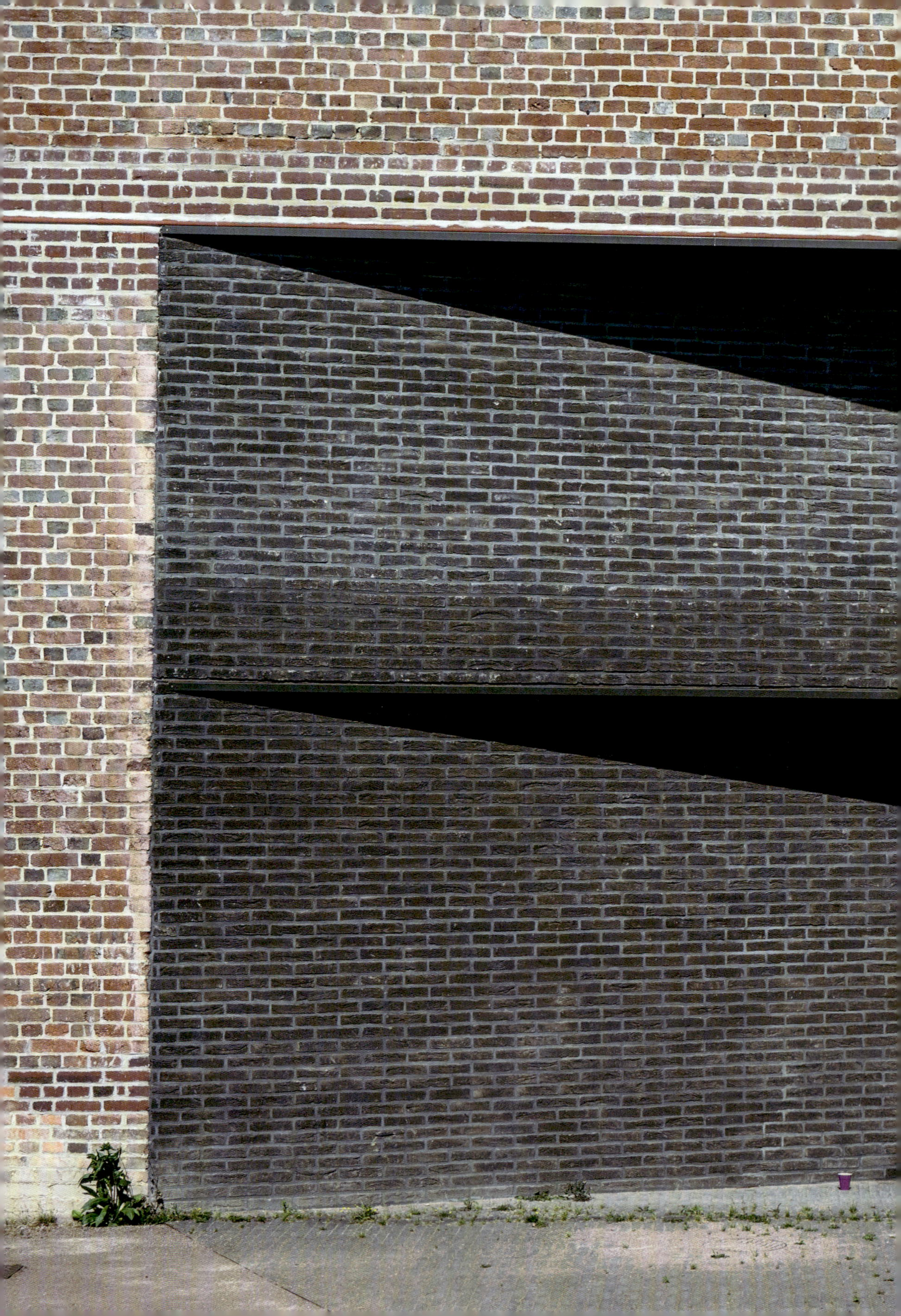

0 1 2 5m

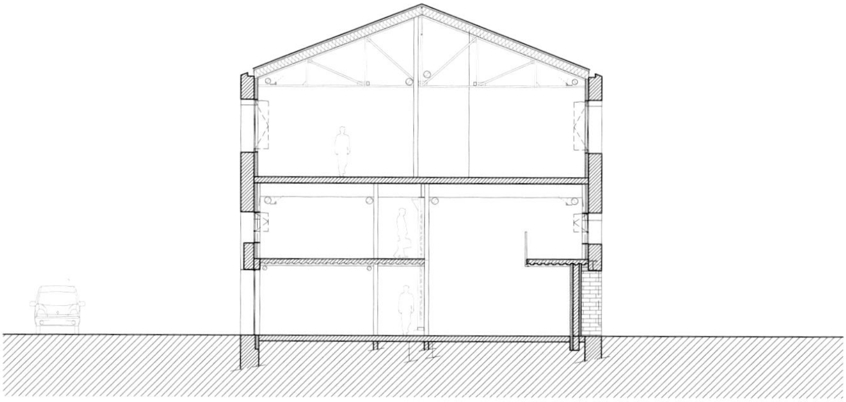

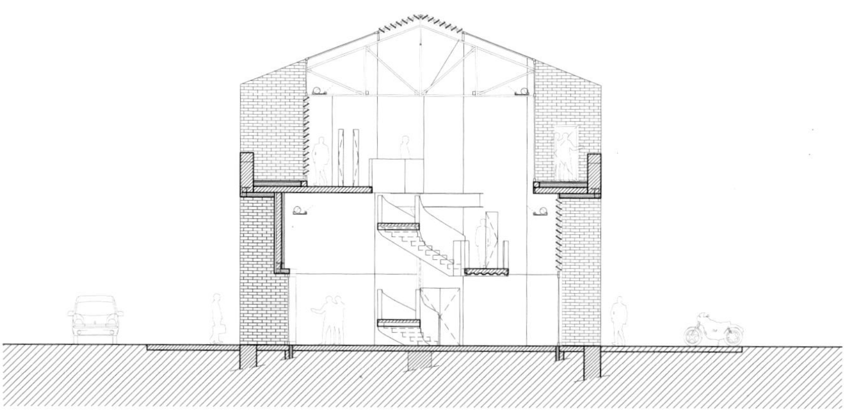

"Space is defined by its use more than by its materiality. Matter comes after material, which is determined by the constructional choice. The project chooses its matter. It has to be rough to be tough. No detail is included that can't stand up to use and time's wear and tear."

« L’espace se qualifie par son usage plus que par sa matérialité. La matière vient après le matériau, qui est déterminé par le choix constructif. Le projet choisit sa matière. Il faut que ce soit fruste pour que ce soit robuste. Tous nos détails sont conçus pour résister aux usages, à l’usure du temps. »

Building site scenes. Cut stone stacked waiting on palettes. Here and there delicate bits of straw sticking out between the sharp edges. The pattern has been drawn exactly, and transferred onto each building element. This one is for the eighth floor, stage left. In a few days the stones will be laid without mortar on beechwood wedges. On the floor of the fifth storey, a hammer and chisel, rarities in today's theatre of architectural operations. The stones will be jointed with plaster. The window sills are gently smoothed with the stone planer – like a caress, a foretaste of the elbows that will lean on them as people contemplate the sky. In the wings, a chance encounter between cut stone and prefabricated concrete. The light rain filters through the layers of the top floor, water streams off the hardhats, the wind is driving the clouds across a sky so low you could touch it. From the outside all you see is the veins and yellow stripes of the Noyant stone, quarried less than a hundred kilometres away. **FL**

Scènes de chantier. Les pierres taillées sont entreposées, attendent leur mise en œuvre sur des palettes. Çà et là, des brins de paille délicats entre les blocs massifs aux arêtes vives. Le calepinage a été dessiné précisément, reporté sur chaque élément à édifier. Ce numéro ira au 8e étage, côté jardin gauche. Dans quelques jours, les pierres seront posées à sec, sur des cales en bois de hêtre. Au sol du 5e, un marteau et un burin, outils devenus rares dans le théâtre des opérations architecturales. Du plâtre fera mortier entre les pierres. Le chemin de fer passé délicatement permettra de poncer les appuis de baie. Comme une caresse, un avant-goût des coudes qui s'appuieront pour regarder le ciel. En coulisses, la rencontre fortuite entre pierre de taille et éléments préfabriqués en béton. Au dernier étage, la pluie fine pénètre entre toutes les épaisseurs, les casques ruissellent, le vent pousse encore les nuages d'un ciel si bas qu'on pourrait le toucher. À l'abri, l'isolant sera posé sur les parois intérieures. De dehors, ne restent que les stries jaunes et les veines de la pierre de Noyant, extraite à moins de cent kilomètres du chantier. **FL**

Apartment building, Avenue Félix-Faure, Paris

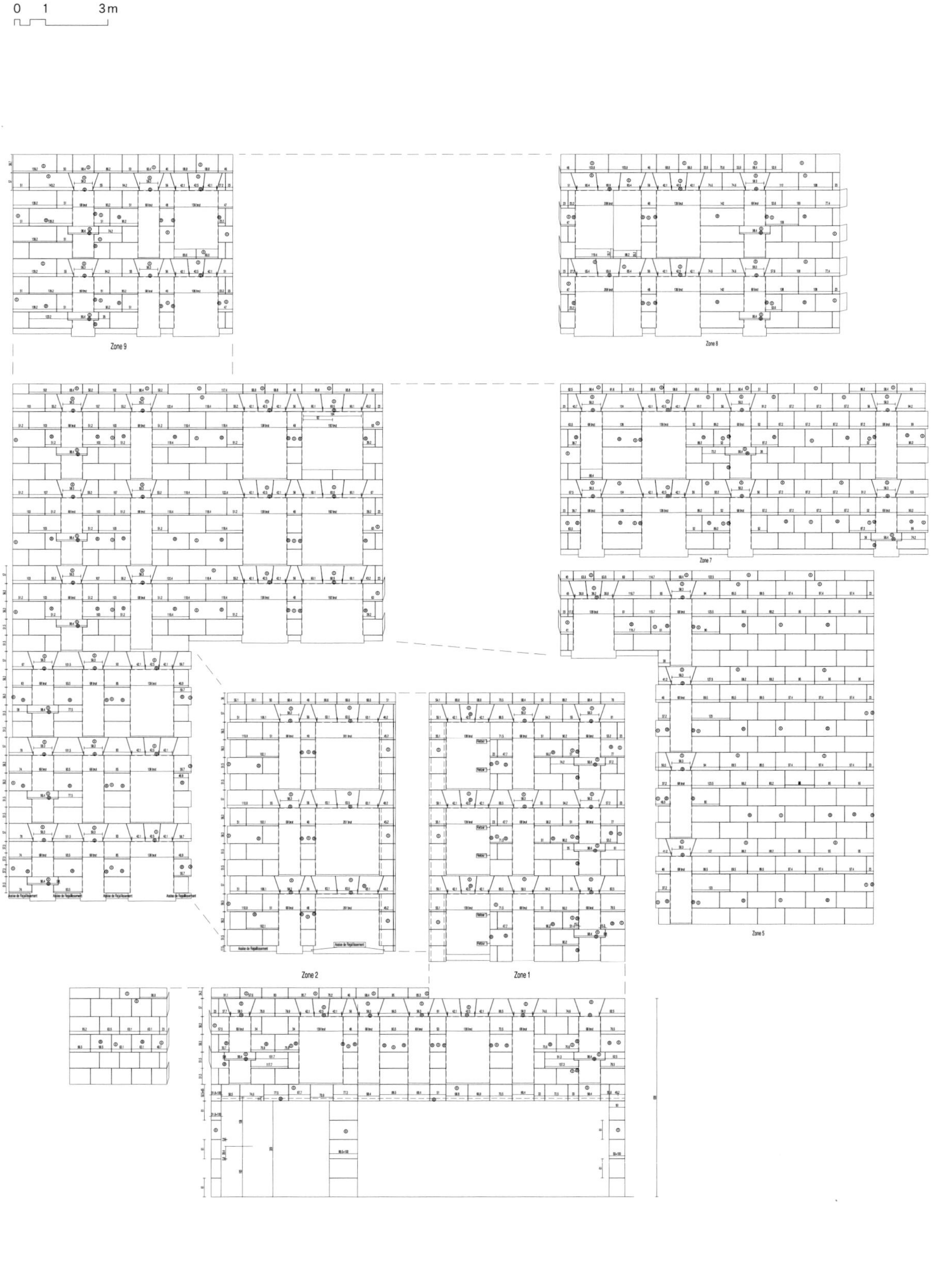
0 1 3m
Zone 9
Zone 8
Zone 7
Zone 5
Zone 2
Zone 1

 Apartment building, Avenue Félix-Faure, Paris

This apartment building is integrated into Avenue Félix-Faure, in Paris's 15th arrondissement, between an eleven-storey 1970s building set back from the street and a two-storey house aligned with the footpath. Taking advantage of this situation, our project also turned its attention to the heart of the block and ideas for multiple orientations. The variations in height, alignment and setback, conceived as a progressive massing, were calculated to preserve the building's linking role and integrate it into its context. The orientation of the apartments hinges on the surrounding buildings, with terraces and loggias offering varied views of the city. Stone, the project's basic material, was chosen for its durability; a historic resource in the Paris basin, it is extracted nearby and requires no processing; and as a solid structural material, it forms an envelope within which the orchestration and dimensions of the openings are adapted to the uses of the different rooms.

Cet immeuble s'inscrit dans la continuité de l'avenue Félix-Faure (15ᵉ), entre un immeuble de onze étages datant des années 1970, en retrait de la rue, et une maison de deux étages alignée sur la rue. Exploitant cette situation en articulation, notre projet se tourne également vers le cœur d'îlot pour proposer des orientations multiples. Les variations de hauteur, d'alignement et de retrait, pensées selon un épannelage progressif, ont été calculées pour conserver à l'édifice son rôle de lien et l'intégrer à son contexte. Les logements s'orientent en fonction des bâtiments environnants ; des terrasses et des loggias offrent des vues variées sur la ville. La pierre, matériau constitutif de ce projet, a été choisie pour sa pérennité. Ressource historique du bassin parisien, elle est extraite à proximité et ne nécessite aucune transformation. Ce matériau massif structurel forme une enveloppe au sein de laquelle le rythme et le dimensionnement des ouvertures s'ajustent aux usages des différentes pièces.

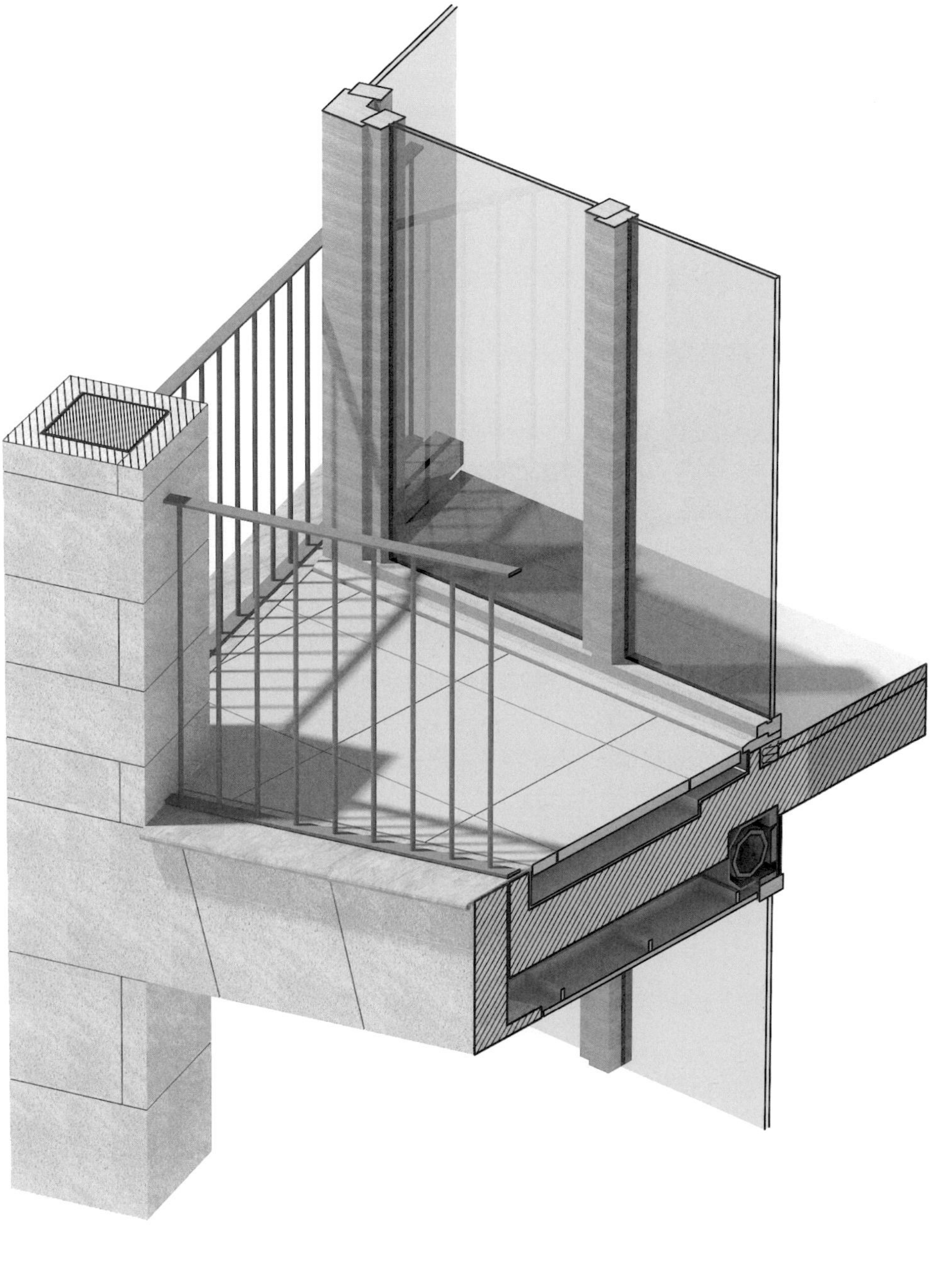

Situated at the corner of Rue Véron and Rue Lepic, in Paris's 18th arrondissement, this project consists of a new corner building attached to an existing, rehabilitated building, both served by a common stairwell. It was a matter of backing-up, enlarging, and constructing an urban edge while keeping the traces of the opening of Montmartre's streets. The temptation to do something spectacular was considerable and it was not easy to stick to the strictly necessary. Ultimately the extension opted for the regularity and simplicity of traditional suburban architecture and its codes: clear demarcation of levels and a typically Parisian coating of white render. Geometrical considerations were moderated to maintain unison with the rehabilitated building, thus providing most apartments with external extensions and views towards the mosaic of roofs at the foot of the Butte Montmartre.

À l'angle des rues Véron et Lepic, dans le 18ᵉ arrondissement, ce projet de logements consiste en un immeuble neuf en angle accolé à un immeuble existant réhabilité, tous deux desservis par une cage d'escalier commune. Il s'agissait de s'adosser, d'agrandir et de construire une arête urbaine tout en gardant les traces de l'histoire du percement des rues de Montmartre. La tentation de faire événement était forte, il n'a pas été facile de s'en tenir au nécessaire. L'extension reprend la régularité et la simplicité des percements de l'architecture faubourienne et adopte les codes de cette dernière : le marquage net entre les niveaux, un revêtement d'enduit blanc typiquement parisien. La géométrie s'infléchit en douceur pour rester à l'unisson du bâtiment réhabilité, offrant ainsi à la plupart des logements des prolongements extérieurs et des vues orientées vers la mosaïque de toits au pied de la butte Montmartre.

la fibre

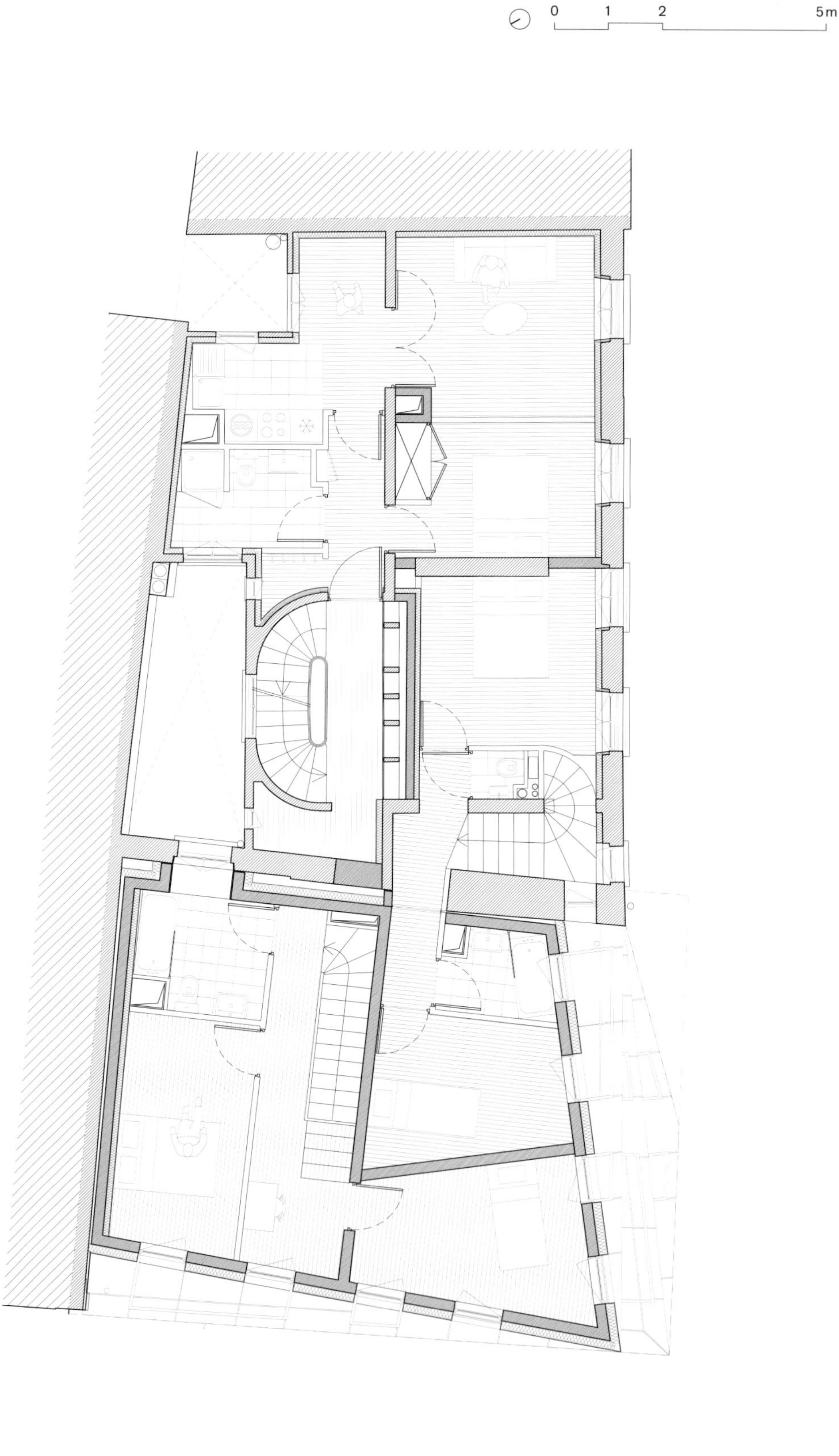
0
1
2
5m

30

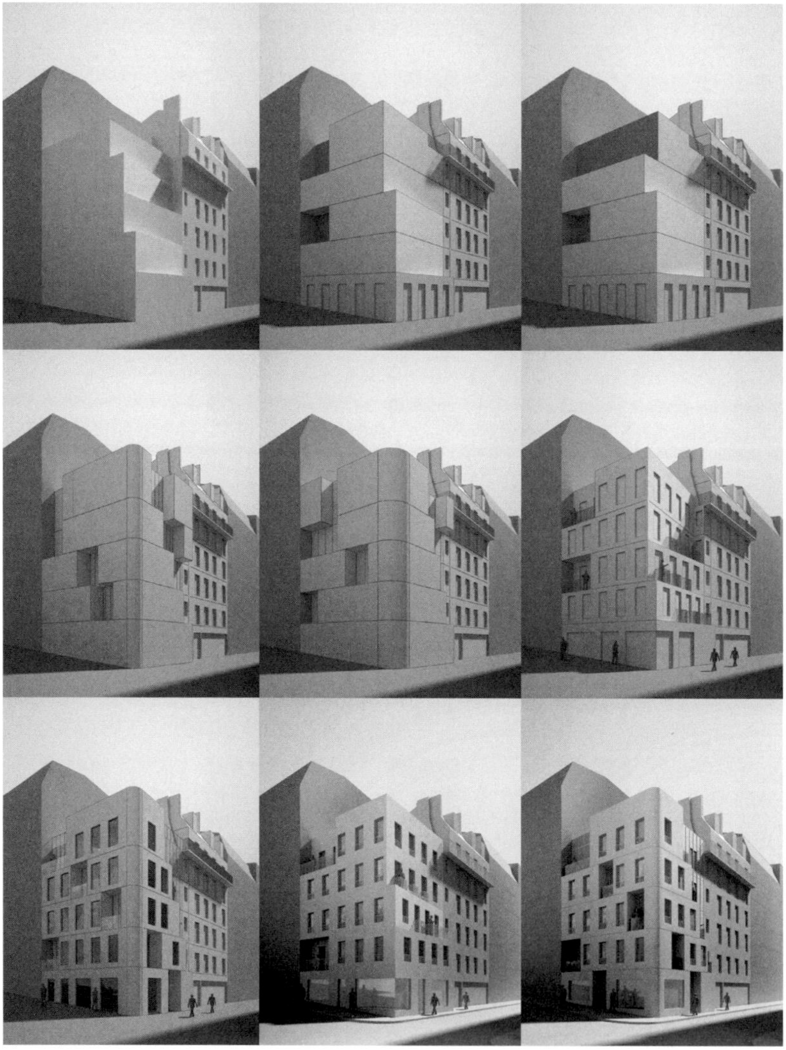

 Apartment building, Rue Véron/Rue Lepic, Paris

PIZZA

This micro-project involved turning a garden pavilion of 12 square metres at floor level into a living space for a teenager. Our client had patiently drawn up an inventory of uses that we then translated into different scenarios aimed at a playful space such as a tree hut, for above-ground living. The space we built revolved around a void, with its uses following one another and intermingling naturally, in a way offering different modes of dwelling. Via its unitary structural material – birch plywood – the result suggests modes of appropriation without imposing them.

Cette micro-architecture prend place dans un ancien pavillon de jardin, construction de 12 mètres carrés au sol à transformer en habitation pour un adolescent. Notre client a réalisé un patient inventaire d'usages que nous avons traduits en différents scénarios pour concevoir un espace ludique, telle une cabane dans les arbres pour habiter dans la hauteur. L'espace construit s'enroule autour du vide ; les usages se succèdent et s'entremêlent naturellement, l'intrication des fonctions offrant différentes manières d'habiter le projet. Cette architecture au matériau unitaire et structurant, le contreplaqué de bouleau, propose des modes d'appropriation sans pour autant les imposer.

CARMY

To maximise shared space via the redesigning of this apartment, cabins and beds had to be optimised and bathrooms made more compact. In a way it was like applying naval architecture to an apartment in the mountains. The empty space freed up in the centre is defined by a big, habitable unit, a curve that sets up a visual dynamic directing the eye towards the bay windows so as to take in the landscape. The contrast between birch plywood and American walnut spells out the functions that activate the space.

Pour générer un maximum d'espaces communs lors du réaménagement de cet appartement, il a fallu optimiser cabines et couchages, et compacter les pièces d'eau. Faire, en quelque sorte, de l'architecture navale appliquée à un appartement à la montagne. Le vide libéré au centre est dessiné par un grand meuble habitable dont la courbe crée une dynamique visuelle qui oriente le regard vers les baies vitrées et permet d'embrasser le paysage. Le contraste entre contreplaqué de bouleau et noyer américain donne à lire les fonctions qui activent l'espace.

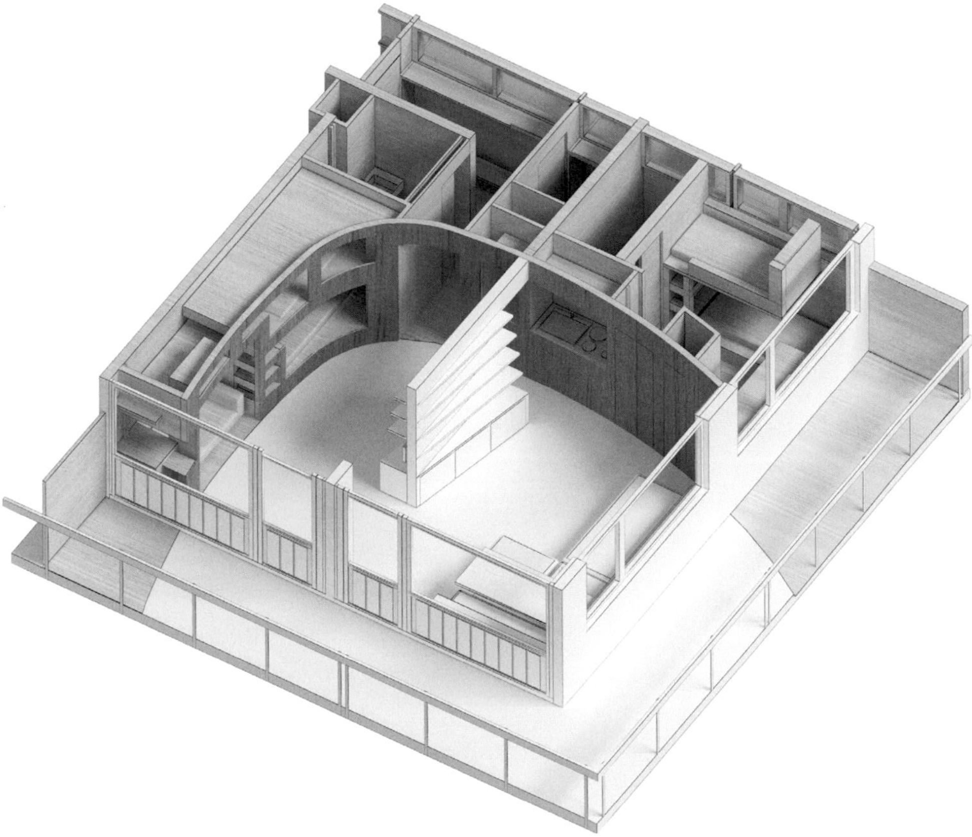

Created by running several maid's rooms together, this top floor apartment comprises a continuous space punctuated with structural items of furniture. Like totems emerging from the ground, they mask or orient uses, creating an interior landscape whose geometry underscores the pitch of the roof and frees up a large diagonal that opens perspectives onto the rooftops of Paris.

Cet appartement sous les toits, fruit de la réunion de plusieurs chambres de bonne, propose un espace continu ponctué d'éléments de mobilier structurants. Comme des totems émergeant du sol, ils masquent ou orientent les usages, créant un paysage intérieur dont la géométrie souligne la pente des rampants de toiture et dégage une grande diagonale qui ouvre des perspectives sur les toits de Paris.

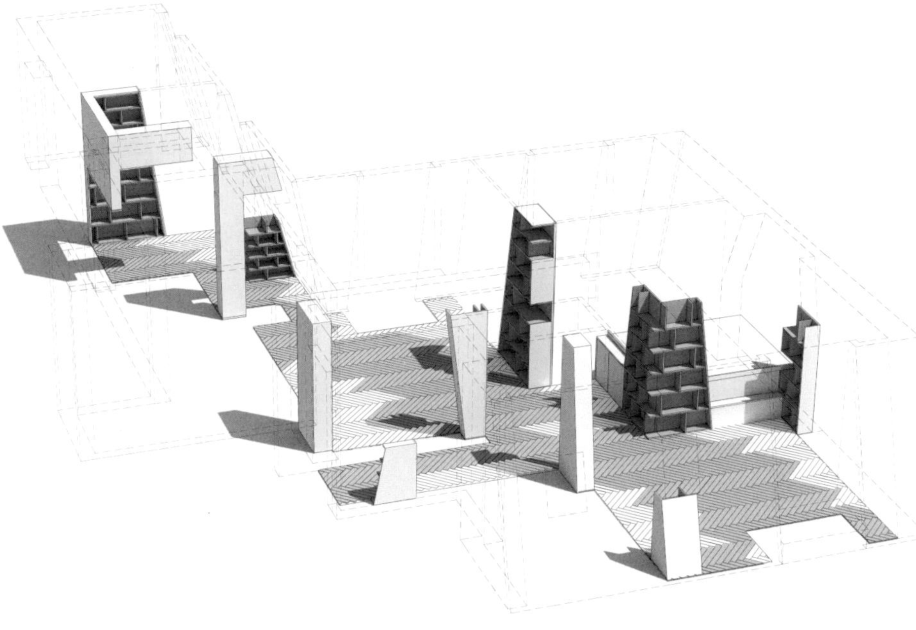

"Heritage isn't there solely to be preserved and enhanced; its meaning has to be restored as well. Modify the extant in order to reveal it. Programme the regeneration of its uses and its meaning. All change seeks to give birth to a new whole at once powerful and coherent. This in a spirit of respect for the extant, rather than in a binary, dualistic confrontation between new and old."

« Le patrimoine n’est pas seulement là pour être conservé et mis en valeur, il faut lui redonner du sens. Modifier l’existant pour le révéler. Programmer le renouvellement de ses usages et de sa signification. Toute transformation cherche à donner naissance à un nouvel ensemble puissant et cohérent, dans le respect de l’existant plutôt que dans une confrontation binaire, duelle, entre neuf et ancien. »

Observing, one Sunday morning in winter. Watching the market being set up, people hurrying by in the cold. Listening to the rattle of the stalls being bolted together. Then the motors of the trucks leaving the square, the shrivelled vegetables being hastily culled by those who can't afford them, before the ballet of the refuse collectors begins. A couple of pigeons stop by, peck at a few crumbs, take off towards the clock tower. The First of May brings big get-togethers: theatre, one-day demonstrations. Then mist, silence, nightfall, streetlamps. You'd like to be able to sit down and watch the kids play. You'd like to be able to cross the street at granny speed. The cars would be ill at ease. Plant grass. Get closer to prior experiments with space. Look at your feet, concentrate, feel, adapt. Install benches for those who'd like to try a ride and impress their little brothers. Boost the authority of the classified monument that's a familiar friend. Naturally. **FL**

Se poster sur la place un dimanche matin d'hiver. Regarder le marché s'installer, les passants se presser dans le froid. Écouter le cliquetis des étals que l'on serre, les moteurs des camions qui abandonnent la place. Les légumes flétris sont glanés de justesse par ceux qui ne peuvent les acheter, juste avant le ballet des éboueurs. Un couple de pigeons s'installe, picore quelques miettes, s'envole vers l'horloge. Les grands rassemblements ont lieu le premier mai : pièces de théâtre, manifestations d'un jour. Et puis la brume, le silence, la nuit, les lampadaires. Il faudra pouvoir s'asseoir pour regarder les enfants jouer. Il faudra pouvoir traverser lentement, à pas de grand-mère. Les voitures se sentiront mal à l'aise. Semer de l'herbe. Se rapprocher d'autres expériences spatiales. Regarder ses pieds, étudier, sentir et adapter. Disposer des bancs pour ceux qui voudraient tenter un *ride* sous les yeux admiratifs des petits frères. Renforcer la puissance du monument classé que l'on tutoie ici. L'air de rien. **FL**

Surroundings of the Familistère, Guise

Abords du familistère, Guise

The aim of rehabilitating the surroundings of the Familistère – a kind of cooperative – in Guise, in Northern France, was to provide a venue for ordinary activities (access to the buildings, motor traffic, etc.) and such less ordinary ones as gatherings, demonstrations and fairs. What we proposed was a free-spirited space that would suggest activities without imposing them. Most important was restoration of the unity of the "social palace" and its integrity. The heart of the site is the square, a statement in its own right and now fluidly functional. Its new covering had to be bricks – echoing the buildings around it – but of a different shade, so as to maintain a nuanced view of the different spaces. This strict material unity is broken by the variety of possible uses: contemplation, crossing, parking, etc. Plant life is colonising the square, creating more of the intimacy favourable to encounters. The urban furniture fits with what goes on in different places. Here and there the ground rises to mark a bus stop or the theatre's access ramp. The mineral quality of the square is complementary to the peninsula garden behind the Familistère.

La réhabilitation des abords du familistère de Guise devait permettre d'accueillir des situations exceptionnelles (rassemblements, manifestations, foires) comme ordinaires (accès aux bâtiments, traversée de véhicules, etc.). Nous avons ainsi proposé un espace permissif, qui suggère des occupations sans les déterminer. Il s'agissait avant tout de restaurer l'unité du « palais social », de lui rendre son intégrité. Au cœur du site se trouve la place, espace manifeste redevenu fluide et fonctionnel. Le revêtement de briques s'est imposé, en écho à la matérialité des bâtiments alentour ; sa teinte est néanmoins différente, afin de préserver une lecture nuancée des espaces. La rigueur du matériau unifié est rompue par la variété des usages proposés (contempler, franchir, stationner…). Les plantations colonisent la place, créant des espaces plus intimes, favorables aux rencontres. Les éléments de mobilier s'ajustent aux pratiques induites par chaque lieu. Le sol se soulève ponctuellement pour marquer les déposes de bus ou bien la rampe d'accès au théâtre. L'espace minéral de la place est complémentaire du jardin de la presqu'île aménagé à l'arrière du familistère.

BUANDERIE - PISCINE

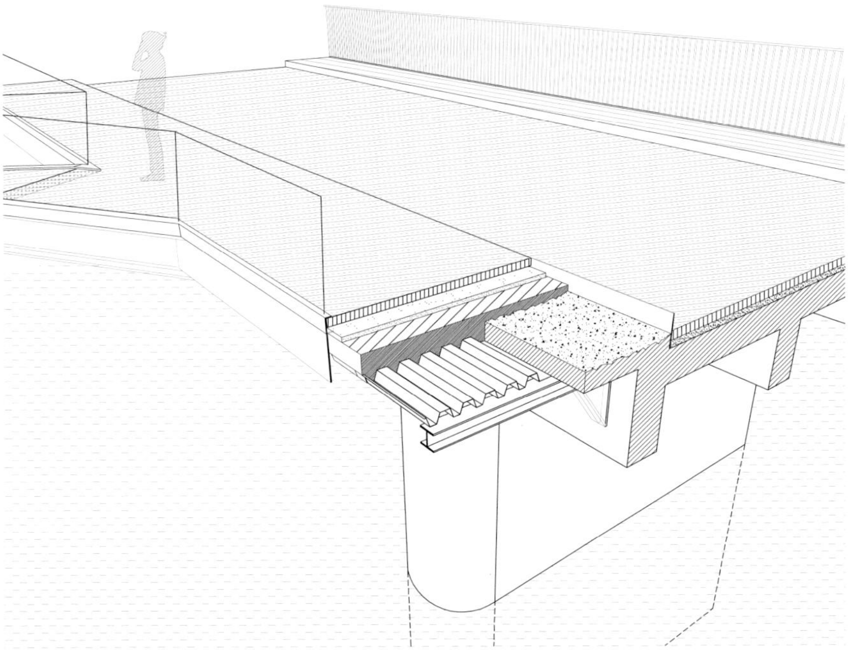

Surroundings of the Familistère, Guise

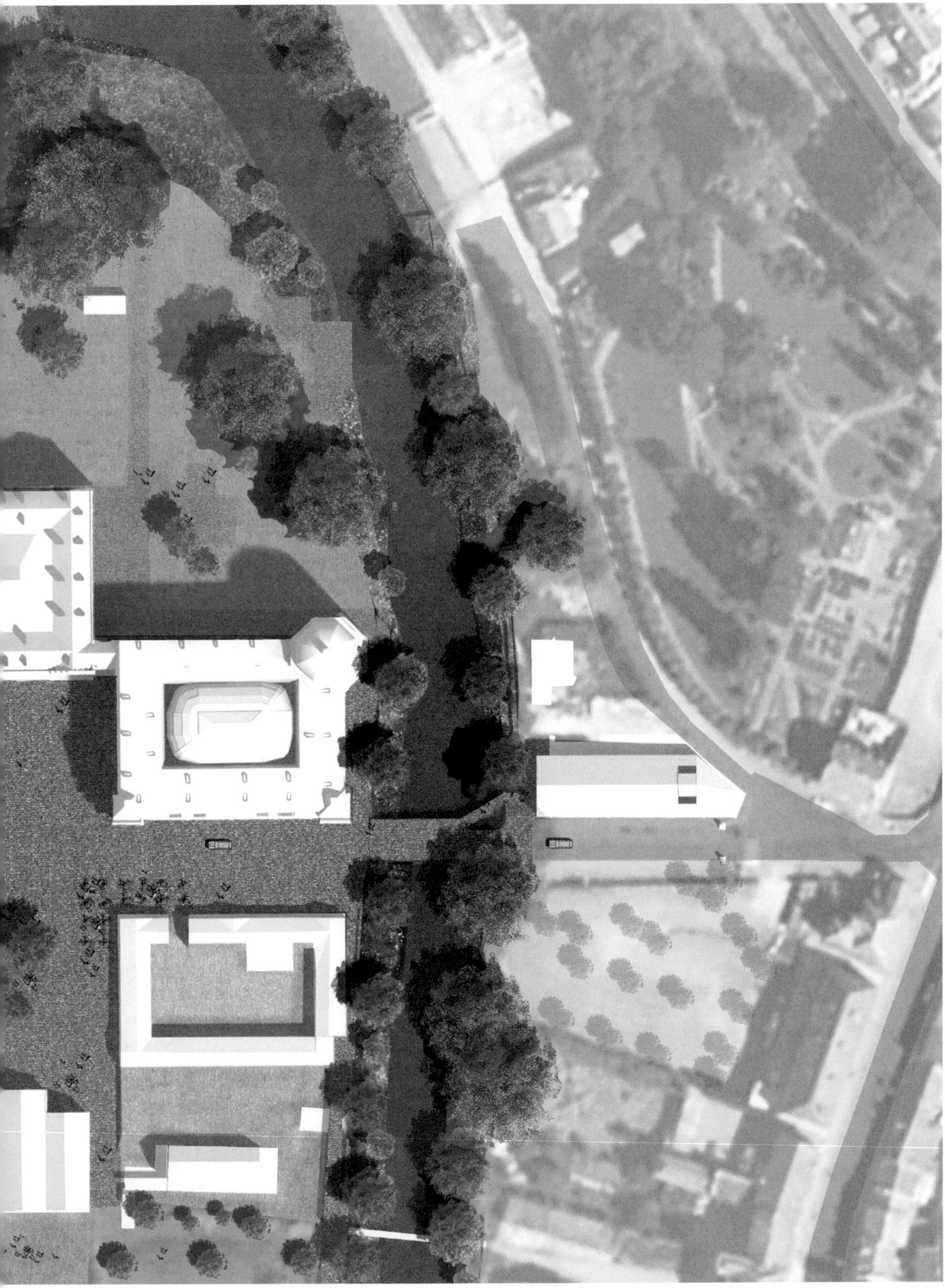

 Surroundings of the cathedral, Évreux

Cathédrale
20

The improvements to the surroundings of Évreux cathedral renew the link between the monument and the city centre around it. Equally divided between vehicles and pedestrians, this space is composed of a single material – stone – which gives the forecourt a unified, almost abstract appearance. However, the handling of stone is refined and adapted according to use and location, in order to create a series of "urban scenes" at the entrances to the cathedral: the ground is sliced, split, smoothed or fractured to guide the pedestrian's step. In front of the west forecourt, the reworked topography generates a powerful link with the Iton, a tributary of the Eure that flows through the city. The restoration of the north portal and our intervention on its forecourt have enabled us to restore this facade to its historical dominance. This programme is part of a larger development project, including a large garden to the south of the cathedral.

L'aménagement des abords de la cathédrale d'Évreux recrée le lien entre le monument et le centre-ville qui l'entoure. Cet espace partagé de manière égale entre véhicules et piétons est constitué d'un seul matériau, la pierre, qui confère un aspect unitaire, quasiment abstrait au parvis. Mais le traitement minéral s'affine et s'adapte en fonction des usages et des lieux afin de créer une série de « scènes urbaines » aux entrées de l'édifice : le sol se découpe, se clive, se lisse ou se fractionne pour guider les pas du piéton. Devant le parvis ouest, la topographie retravaillée génère un lien fort avec l'Iton, affluent de l'Eure qui traverse la ville. La restauration du portail nord et notre intervention sur son parvis ont permis de rendre à cette façade sa prépondérance historique. Ce programme s'inscrit dans un projet d'aménagement plus vaste, comptant notamment un grand jardin au sud de la cathédrale.

Surroundings of the cathedral, Évreux

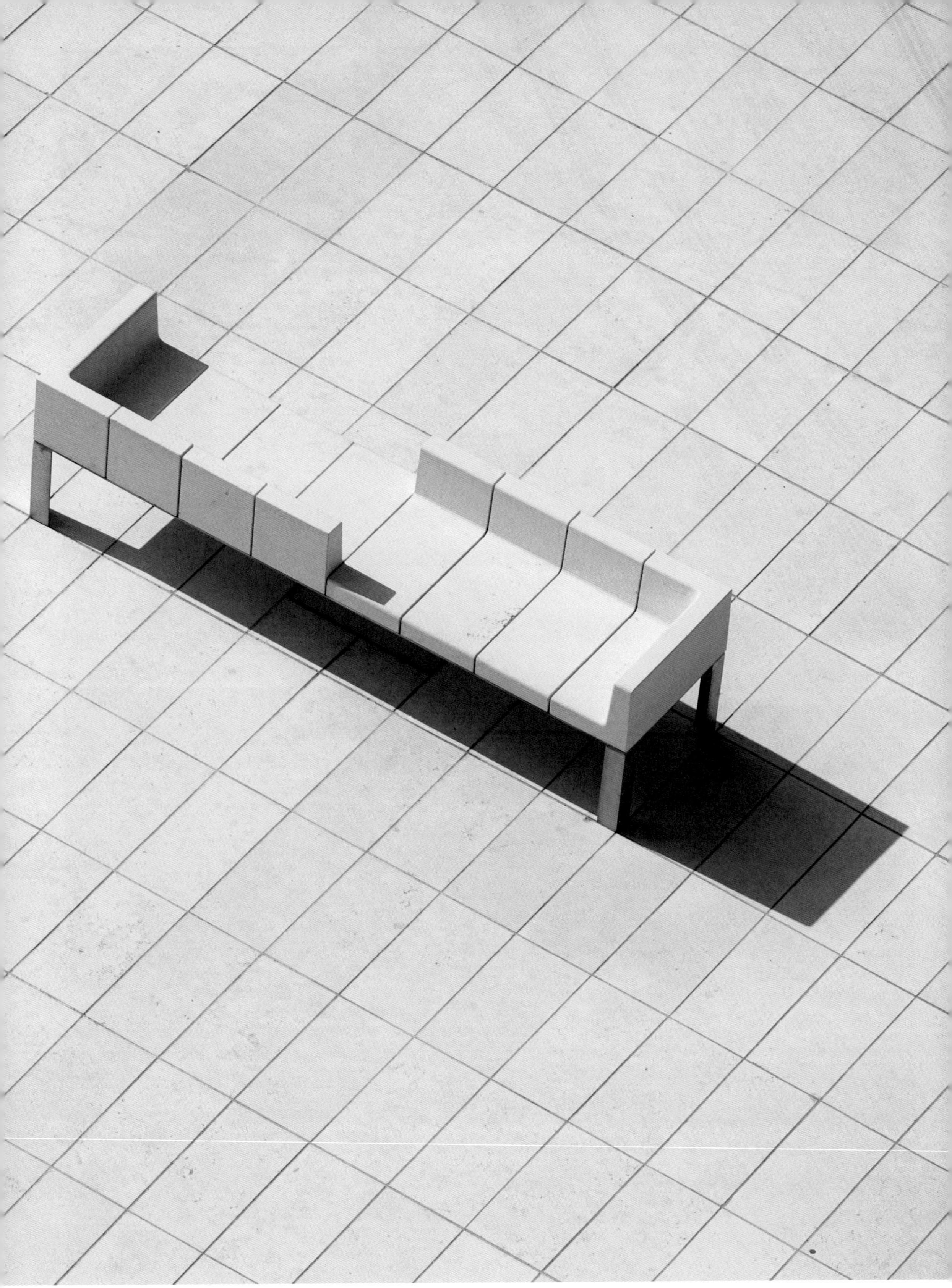

Surroundings of the cathedral, Évreux

"We don't put too much affect into a project. Our approach is an oscillation between the commitment that ensures direction and the trust that leaves elbow room. Starting out with no competitions and relying on direct commissions, we've acquired the habit of justifying ourselves. Of explaining and reassuring, demonstrating our hypotheses and being ready to see part of each project up for discussion."

« Nous ne plaçons pas trop d'affects dans un projet. Notre démarche est une oscillation entre s'impliquer pour orienter et savoir confier pour laisser du champ. Nous avons pris l'habitude de rendre des comptes dès nos premières commandes, directes, sans concours. D'expliquer et de rassurer, de montrer des hypothèses et, de fait, d'accepter de voir une partie du projet mise en discussion. »

Slow but sure: the ethnographer and the field survey
Miguel Mazeri

Miguel Mazeri is an architect, holder of a PhD in social anthropology, and a graduate of EHESS (Paris), the School of Advanced Studies in the Social Sciences. His research bears on the evolution of relations between humans and the environment as seen through an ethnographic filter. A teacher-researcher at the School of Art and Design in Le Mans, he oversees the Design and Territory master's there and is co-director of the research programme "Hospitality in the Anthropocene: towards a reactive approach to territory through design". He is also a dissertation supervisor at the National School of Industrial Design (ENSCI-Les Ateliers) in Paris and a consultant for contracting authorities and prime contractors.

I regularly step in at the h2o agency at the concept design stage or for the urban and architectural analysis. This involves an initial programme for the places scheduled for intervention by the architects: sometimes the nature and configuration of the project call for a meticulous social and environmental diagnosis. For the refurbishing of the West Guyana hospital complex at Saint-Laurent-du-Maroni, for example, the members of the agency decided that, given the project's social and urban implications, it would be a good idea to back up their health assessment of the buildings with programmed and spontaneous interviews. From the outset this standard practice of recording conversations makes for a slow process of maturation of opinions and ideas, a climate of intelligent debate, a pool of standpoints which are open-ended, but stored in a way that discreetly but vitally adds up to a history of ordinary folk. Out of the interview technique there arises an authentic ecology of attentiveness to the project and the diversity of the participants.

Independently of the project's issues, the presence of an anthropologist at the agency and the execution of a study in the field rely on a kind of pact and a real willingness on the part of the architects to be surprised and contaminated by knowledge modes other than those habitually associated with projects; to bank on the usefulness of bringing personal forms of observation into play; to accept the emergence of contradictions in the discussion; and to preserve the independence and impartiality of the practical method. My being there as an anthropologist for the architects helped reinforce their working knowledge, ensuring practical attentiveness to people and closeness to their sources, while at the same time foregrounding individuals' issues and affiliations.

As a rule, pre-project studies result in the accumulation of data – topographic, legal, economic, historic, infrastructural and cultural – on the place in question. They also include an exact account of the relevant buildings in the study sector and of the applicable urban planning regulations. A flora and fauna health report may also be requested. The sociological aspect is frequently brought up and can be quickly dealt with by adding in a statistical table taken from the appropriate government data bank. The resultant picture – fairly general, distant and impersonal – struggles to provide a clear and meaningful description of an ambiance.

Calling in an anthropologist for the sociological aspect enables other forms of investigation – notably in the field – by opening the study up to the sentient, changing world of city dwellers and their ways of living, of occupying public space, of moving about or staying put, of using their streets and boulevards. Only an architectural team at once determined and demanding (and convinced of the need for a prior harvesting of human reactions) can fully actualise the sociological by restoring its experiential aspect. This often revamps the statistical data and the points of view that go with it, which is what underlay the renovation of the social housing blocks on Rue Félix-Terrier in Paris's 20th arrondissement, the Reuilly barracks in the 12th arrondissement and the Guyanese hospital complex mentioned above. "Observation is a means of skirting statistical pitfalls", as French sociologists Michel Pinçon and Monique Pinçon-Charlot point out in their aptly named *Paris, quinze promenades sociologiques.*

The brevity of initial programmes and urban diagnoses might seem contradictory in relation to the time required by the field enquiry. But at the same time this temporal constraint establishes the rules and in spite of everything generates other investigative formats and strategies.

The ethnographic approach is rarely referred to in calls for tenders, probably because it is harder to identify in terms of its methodology and its purpose as seen by the client. As if understanding a place and theorising its transformation required no more than the measurement of its dimensions and materiality, a scrupulous inventory of the rules and regulations, immersion in architectural and urban history, and meticulous noting of what's overtly wrong with the way it's built. As if all there was to see in its material wear and tear was the trace of a life drawing to a close and awaiting replacement – never that of a necessary revival requiring our consent as a starting point. Thus finding a visible, intelligible form of the social in our knowledge of the city falls to the ethnographer. Consideration of how this element of the social, which dwells in, forms and informs the city, must be taken into account despite its diffuseness, falls to all of us. It's up to architects to call for this and promote the cause.

The ethnographer – especially in his dealings with the architect – cannot claim exclusive rights to focusing on living conditions for humans and, more generally, in the natural environment. Nonetheless his specific role and his method mean he foregrounds these conditions, systematically implementing them and updating them in and via investigation in the field. This updating takes time and it may be here, in substance, that the ethnographer gains in value. Evaluation of a place – "consideration" would be a more accurate way of putting it – requires repeated activity: periods of observation founded on an intuitive sensory depth of field that sometimes needs to be markedly open-ended and fluctuating if the banal forces underlying the functioning of a place are to be noted and understood. This practice requires a degree of tolerance on the part of the architects, plus a tacit acceptance of the approach that lets it find its place and set up positive echoes within the team. The results are not instantaneous and can sometimes appear minor, but it's now up to the ethnographer to show how certain data in this minor mode – a tag on a wall, grass sprouting through the footpath, a pedestrian expressing annoyance – are also functionally and relationally symptomatic of local usage.

Via this immersion in the daily life of a neighbourhood, ethnography – at least in the form I advocate for urban architectural ventures – sets out with no preconceptions to describe residents' lives inasfar as they involve statements: deeds and actions, usages and practices, challenges and confidences.

Methodologically the ethnographer de facto displaces his investigation into a conversational mode in which spoken exchange breaks down the barriers between points of view. Drawing (because he's curious) on the variety of available human resources, he switches between more or less close-up contexts ranging from vox pop talking heads to more conventional interviews: experiences are shared and discussed in a deliberately multifaceted situation closer to that of observer/commentator than of the more categorical investigator. The field study is based on a sharing of sensibilities and the empirical data gathered in the course of this process can vary from the extremely spontaneous to the relatively structured. The ethnographer is looking to the man in the street as an actor, not as a mere figure.

The ethnographer's stock in trade is his knowledge of daily urban life: he scrutinises its rhythms, routines, habits – and its breaking of the rules. In this regard his presence in an architecture agency silently ensures the presence of the users as well. It's not his business to represent them – although this may happen – but rather to make them a core force for determination and aspiration within the project. The ethnographer's workspace is as much social as architectural and urban. He is more or less hemmed in by the study and the experience of dwelling in a territory. He observes the way the residents use the resources of the city: in a sense he measures their individual usage skills, but is also trying to find out how these are acquired. The resources are unfairly distributed, not always visible, not always accessible, and variously open to appropriation according to generation, cultural background and social affiliations. If a given material resource exists for all within the city, the ethnographer must be attentive to its conditions of access. To note its existence is not enough: he must also explain its structural elements and ensure modes of access for all.

Through these formal features, though, the city implicitly constructs more or less satisfying modes of conduct for residents. The study in the field attempts to cover a dual objective whose components – we could term them "resident relevance" (conscious use of the city's material and immaterial resources) and "urban relevance" (the implicit impact of urban forms on ways of inhabiting) – interact constantly in the iterative experience of the day-to-day.

The role of the ethnographer for the duration of the project has to do not only with the collection of empirical data, but also with their correlation, interpretation and ultimate diffusion. In particular he must ensure that certain intuitive data not systematically subject to written or graphic interpretation are brought to the attention of the architecture team. The feeling of well-being or malaise emanating from a situation or place can sometimes be relatively muted, but it must remain discernible and open to debate.

The graphic language of field ethnography is an open-ended exploratory domain, with plans and maps serving as elements of a shared language that ethnography can use with no sacrifice of meaning. Photos with captions, drawings stamped with a time and date: these are the ethnographer's visual backup. Handwritten captions are plentiful. Maps can help situate observations and inventory items on a plan – streetlamps, trees, benches and other urban furniture – and pin down the fleeting impressions gained on foot.

The ethnographer's zone of investigation is often vast. For example, the study of the "HBM" social housing on Rue Félix-Terrier, originally intended to last a few days, evolved into a month-long HBM inventory of the Paris ring road. The Reuilly barracks project also triggered observation extending to the area around the 12th arrondissement. The governing idea is that whatever the place you get there from somewhere, and whatever the case these broader observations enrich the narrower ones.

The results of the study in the field accompany a collective appraisal and restore the focus to the human, independently of all other global economic constraints. Walking, time and listening structure the ethnographer's fieldwork: ensuring the repeated presence that attracts attention without being alarming; learning from chance encounters as much as from formally arranged ones; staying just as attentive to remarks overheard in the street and outside the lift as to the more solemn utterances of people's living rooms.

Fieldwork means engaging with contrasts, noting discord, spotting nuances. During the visits to the apartments in the Boulevard Davout HBM operation, invaluable information was picked up in this way and written down alphabetically under the heading "They said". This method quickly proved useful for the most frequent occurrences: appropriation, artists, associations, burglaries, cellars, common areas, gardens, heating, neighbourhood image, neighbours, renovations, schools, shops, social solidarity, sports facilities, water damage.

"He was standing behind a window gazing through the fine green filter of the garden air to the brownish street beyond, and for the last ten minutes he had been ticking off on his stopwatch the passing cars, trucks, trolleys, and pedestrians, whose faces were washed out by the distance, timing everything whirling past that he could catch in the net of his eye. He was gauging their speeds, their angles, all the living forces of mass hurtling past that drew the eye to follow them like lightning, holding on, letting go, forcing the attention for a split second to resist, to snap, to leap in pursuit of the next item… Then, after doing the arithmetic in his head for a while, he slipped the watch back into his pocket with a laugh and decided to stop all this nonsense. If all those leaps of attention, fleeings of eye muscles, fluctuations of the psyche, if all the effort it takes for a man just to hold himself upright within the flow of traffic on a busy street could be measured, he thought – as he toyed with calculating the incalculable – the grand total would surely dwarf the energy needed by Atlas to hold up the world, and one could then estimate the enormous undertaking it is nowadays merely to be a person who does nothing at all."

Robert Musil, *The Man without Qualities*, trans. Sophie Wilkins and Burton Pike (London: Picador, 2017).

Le pas (lent) de l'ethnographe : le relevé de terrain
Miguel Mazeri

Miguel Mazeri est architecte et docteur en anthropologie sociale, diplômé de l'École des hautes études en sciences sociales. Ses travaux portent sur l'évolution des rapports entre l'homme et l'environnement vus par le prisme d'une lecture ethnographique du monde social. Enseignant-chercheur à l'École supérieure d'art et de design du Mans, il coordonne le master « Design et territoire » et est co-responsable du programme de recherche « Hospitalité à l'ère de l'anthropocène : pour une approche sensible des territoires par le design ». Il est également directeur de mémoires à l'École nationale supérieure de création industrielle (ENSCI-Les Ateliers) à Paris. Miguel exerce en parallèle en tant que consultant auprès de maîtrises d'œuvre et d'ouvrage.

J'interviens régulièrement au sein de l'agence h2o, dans le cadre d'études préalables au projet ou au sein du diagnostic architectural et urbain. Il s'agit de mener une étude de définition des lieux dans lesquels les architectes vont devoir intervenir. En effet, parfois, la nature et la configuration du projet appellent à un diagnostic social et environnemental pointilleux. Pour la requalification du centre hospitalier de l'Ouest guyanais à Saint-Laurent-du-Maroni par exemple, l'agence jugeait utile, eu égard aux enjeux humains et métropolitains du projet, d'adosser à leur mission d'expertise sanitaire des bâtiments un espace d'entretiens programmés et libres. Institutionnaliser le recours à des temps de parole enregistrés permet d'entreprendre dès le départ du projet un lent travail de maturation des opinions et des idées, de faire naître un espace d'entretiens de qualité, de constituer une réserve commune d'opinions qui pourra évoluer, mais qui grâce à l'archivage tisse de manière discrète, et pourtant essentielle, l'histoire des communs. Par l'entremise de l'entretien, c'est toute une écologie de l'attention portée au projet et à la diversité de ses acteurs qui se met en place.

Indépendamment des enjeux du projet, la présence d'un anthropologue au sein d'une agence et la réalisation d'une étude de terrain reposent sur une sorte de pacte et une réelle volonté de la part des architectes de se laisser surprendre et contaminer par d'autres modes comptables de savoirs habituellement propres au projet, de parier sur l'utilité de faire advenir des formes sensibles d'observation, d'assumer l'émergence de formes contradictoires dans le débat et de préserver l'indépendance et l'impartialité de la démarche de terrain. Ma présence d'anthropologue contribue à renforcer auprès des architectes les savoirs d'usage. Elle assure au sein de l'équipe une vigilance concrète à hauteur d'homme et une proximité avec ses sources. Elle met en présence les problématiques de chacun et les appartenances.

Les études préalables au projet sont habituellement constituées d'un certain nombre de données topographiques, législatives, économiques, historiques, infrastructurelles et culturelles sur le lieu étudié. Elles comprennent aussi un relevé précis des bâtiments concernés par le secteur d'étude ainsi que les règles d'urbanisme applicables. Un relevé sanitaire de la flore et de la faune peut être également demandé. Le volet sociologique est souvent évoqué et peut rapidement être satisfait par l'ajout d'un tableau statistique recopié d'une base de données appropriée (de type INSEE/INED). Une image sera donnée, assez générale, distante et impersonnelle, qui peinera à faire sens pour décrire précisément une ambiance.

Recourir à un anthropologue pour répondre au volet sociologique permet d'autres formes d'investigation, notamment celle du terrain, en ouvrant l'étude au domaine vivant et changeant des usagers de la ville, à leurs manières de l'habiter, d'occuper l'espace public, de circuler ou de séjourner, de pratiquer la rue et le boulevard. Seule une maîtrise d'œuvre volontaire, exigeante (et convaincue de la nécessité d'une récolte préalable des sensibilités humaines) permet de faire exister pleinement ce volet sociologique en lui redonnant une forme expérientielle. Les données statistiques et les points de vue associés s'en trouvent souvent dépoussiérés. C'est le travail qui a été mené sur la rénovation des HBM de la rue Félix-Terrier dans le 20e arrondissement de Paris, la réhabilitation de la caserne de Reuilly dans le 12e arrondissement de Paris ou encore la reconversion du centre hospitalier susmentionné. « L'observation permet de déjouer les pièges des amalgames statistiques », rappellent les sociologues Michel Pinçon et Monique Pinçon-Charlot dans un livre bien nommé : *Paris, quinze promenades sociologiques.*

Le temps court alloué aux études de définition ou aux diagnostics urbains pourrait paraître contradictoire avec celui nécessaire à l'enquête de terrain. Mais c'est également cette contrainte temporelle qui, en fixant les règles, va faire émerger d'autres formats et stratégies d'enquête, malgré tout.

La démarche ethnographique est rare dans les appels d'offres, probablement parce que moins identifiable dans sa méthode et dans sa finalité de la part de la maîtrise d'ouvrage. Comme si, pour comprendre un lieu et faire l'hypothèse de sa transformation, il ne fallait compter que sur le relevé dimensionnel et matériel d'un espace, faire l'inventaire consciencieux des réglementations, se plonger dans l'histoire architecturale et urbaine, noter scrupuleusement les désordres observés sur le bâti. Comme s'il ne fallait voir dans l'usure des matériaux que la trace d'une fin de vie à remplacer et jamais celle d'un renouvellement nécessaire à consentir et sur lequel s'appuyer. Trouver une forme visible et intelligible de la part sociale dans les savoirs sur la ville incombe donc à l'ethnographe. Penser que cette part sociale qui habite la ville, la forme et l'informe doit être prise en compte, malgré son caractère diffus, incombe à tous. Que les architectes le requièrent et s'en fassent les prescripteurs !

L'ethnographe ne peut s'octroyer à lui seul, notamment vis-à-vis de l'architecte, le monopole de l'intérêt porté aux conditions de vie des humains et plus largement du vivant mais, de par sa spécificité et sa méthode, il fait de ces conditions un sujet de premier plan et fait systématiquement le choix de les mobiliser en les remettant à jour dans et par l'enquête de terrain. Cette mise à jour prend du temps et c'est peut-être là, en substance, que l'ethnographe construit sa plus-value. L'évaluation d'un lieu – sa « considération » serait plus juste, puisque c'est de cela qu'il s'agit – demande une pratique répétée, des temps d'observation qui reposent sur des focales sensibles et intuitives parfois très ouvertes et flottantes afin de consigner et de comprendre les ressorts très ordinaires de fonctionnement d'un lieu. Ce procédé demande de la part de la maîtrise d'œuvre une certaine bienveillance et l'acceptation tacite de se laisser imprégner par la démarche afin qu'elle puisse trouver sa place et construire un mode de résonance positif au sein de l'équipe. Les résultats ne sont pas instantanés et peuvent parfois paraître mineurs. C'est alors à l'ethnographe de montrer comment ce mode mineur de certaines données (un tag sur un mur, une touffe d'herbe sur le trottoir, l'agacement d'un piéton, etc.) est aussi un symptôme fonctionnel et relationnel des usagers du lieu.

En s'immergeant dans la vie quotidienne d'un quartier, l'ethnographie (du moins celle que je revendique au sein de la maîtrise d'œuvre urbaine et architecturale) s'attelle sans parti pris à décrire les vies habitantes au plus près de leurs modes d'énonciation de faits et de gestes, d'usages et de pratiques, d'interpellations et de confidences.

De par sa méthode, l'ethnographe fait reposer *de facto* son projet d'enquête sur un mode conversationnel où la parole circule et vient décloisonner les points de vue. En s'appuyant sur la diversité des ressources humaines à sa portée (curieux de ce qui se présente à lui), en alternant la possibilité de liens distants ou plus rapprochés, du micro-trottoir à l'entretien plus formel, les expériences sont partagées et discutées dans un rôle volontairement protéiforme qui s'apparente davantage à celui d'observateur et de commentateur qu'à celui plus univoque d'enquêteur. L'étude de terrain se fonde sur un commun partage des sensibilités. C'est dans ce processus que les données empiriques se récoltent de manière parfois très spontanée, parfois plus réfléchie. C'est l'agir-piéton plus que l'être-piéton que l'ethnographe convoite.

L'apprentissage du quotidien de la ville constitue le fonds de commerce de l'ethnographe : scruter les rythmes, les régularités, les habitudes et ses entorses. En ce sens, sa présence au sein d'une agence assure silencieusement celle des usagers. Non que sa tâche soit de les représenter, encore que, mais plutôt de les faire exister comme volonté et désir au centre du projet. Le terrain de l'ethnographe est un espace social autant qu'un espace architectural et urbain. Il est plus ou moins bordé par l'étude et par l'expérience habitante d'un territoire. Il observe la façon dont les habitants mobilisent les ressources de la ville. En un sens, il mesure les compétences d'usage de chacun, mais cherche aussi à savoir comment celles-ci s'acquièrent. Les ressources sont inéquitablement réparties, pas toujours visibles, pas toujours accessibles et diversement appropriables selon les âges de la vie, les milieux culturels, les appartenances sociales. Si une ressource existe matériellement pour tous dans l'espace de la ville, l'ethnographe doit être attentif à ses conditions d'accès. Répertorier son existence n'est pas suffisant, encore faut-il en expliquer les supports et en assurer les modes d'accès pour tous.

Mais par ces formes, la ville construit implicitement des conduites plus ou moins satisfaisantes pour les habitants. L'enquête de terrain tente de relever un double objectif que nous pourrions nommer « le faire habitant » (l'usage conscient des ressources matérielles et immatérielles de la ville) et le « faire ville » (l'impact implicite des formes de la ville sur les manières de l'habiter) brassés constamment dans l'expérience itérative de la vie quotidienne.

La place de l'ethnographe pendant la durée de vie du projet se situe aussi bien du côté de la collecte de données empiriques que du côté de la traduction, restitution et, *in fine*, diffusion de ces données. Il doit veiller notamment à ce que l'existence de certaines données intuitives qui ne trouvent pas systématiquement d'interprétation graphique ou écrite puisse faire l'objet de considération de la part de la maîtrise d'œuvre. Le sentiment de bien-être ou de mal-être que dégage l'expérience d'une situation, d'un lieu peut rester parfois relativement inexpressif, mais doit demeurer audible et discutable.

Le langage graphique de l'ethnographie de terrain est un domaine exploratoire ouvert. Le recours au plan et à la cartographie forme un élément de langage commun que l'ethnographie peut facilement utiliser sans sacrifier ses éléments de sens. Les photos accompagnées de légendes, des dessins estampillés d'une date et d'une heure constituent les supports visuels de l'ethnographe. Les légendes sont nombreuses. Le recours à la cartographie permet de restituer les observations, d'inventorier les objets dans la ville (les lampadaires, les arbres, le mobilier urbain comme les bancs, etc.) sur un plan et de redresser les impressions fuyantes de la marche.

L'espace d'investigation de l'ethnographe est très souvent surdimensionné. Ainsi l'étude prévue sur quelques jours des HBM rue Félix-Terrier s'est-elle transformée en inventaire des HBM de la ceinture parisienne pendant un mois. Le projet de la caserne de Reuilly a lui aussi fait l'objet d'une observation étendue jusqu'au pourtour du 12e arrondissement. C'est toujours l'idée qu'un lieu, on y arrive bien de quelque part et que de toutes les façons, ces observations élargies viendront enrichir celles plus resserrées.

Le résultat de l'enquête de terrain accompagne une réflexion d'ensemble. Il remet au centre la perspective humaine indépendamment de toute autre contrainte d'économie globale du projet. La marche, le temps, l'écoute sont les éléments qui structurent le travail de terrain. Compter sur sa propre présence répétée pour attirer indirectement sur soi l'attention, sans effrayer ; se laisser instruire par des situations de rencontres fortuites autant que par celles programmées, redoubler d'attention vis-à-vis des petites phrases glanées dans la rue et au pied des immeubles autant que vis-à-vis des messages plus solennels portés dans les salons. Le travail de terrain consiste à investir les contrastes, relever les discordances, situer les différents sons de cloche. Sur l'opération de réhabilitation d'HBM du boulevard Davout, lors des visites des logements, de précieux témoignages furent ainsi relevés et retranscrits dans un abécédaire, « ils ont dit », forme qui se trouva très vite opérante pour remonter les occurrences les plus utilisées : appropriation, artistes, associations, cambriolages, caves, chauffage, commerces, dégâts des eaux, écoles, enfants, équipements sportifs, image (du quartier), jardin, lien social, parties communes, travaux, voisins.

« Debout derrière l'une de fenêtres, il regardait la rue brunâtre à travers le filtre vert tendre de l'air du jardin et comptait depuis dix minutes, montre en main, les autos, les voitures, les tramways et les visages, délavés par la distance, des piétons qui emplissaient le filet du regard de leur hâte mousseuse ; il évaluait les vitesses, les angles, le dynamisme des masses en mouvement les unes devant les autres qui, le temps d'un éclair, attirent l'œil, le retiennent et le relâchent et qui, pendant une durée échappant à toute mesure, contraignent l'attention à s'appuyer sur elles, à s'en détacher pour sauter sur la suivante et se jeter à ses trousses ; enfin, après avoir calculé un instant de tête, il remit sa montre dans sa poche, éclata de rire et constata qu'il avait perdu son temps. Si l'on pouvait mesurer les sauts de l'attention, l'activité des muscles oculaires, les oscillations pendulaires de l'âme et tous les efforts qu'un homme doit s'imposer pour se maintenir debout dans le flot de la rue, on obtiendrait probablement une grandeur en comparaison de laquelle la force dont Atlas a besoin pour porter le monde n'est rien, et l'on pourrait mesurer l'extraordinaire activité déployée de nos jours par celui-là même qui ne fait rien. »

Robert Musil, *L'Homme sans qualités*, Vienne, 1930-1943.

The transformation of this former army barracks had to be exemplary in terms of respect for context and interaction with the various publics concerned. Our strategy was a flexible one, based on the principle of an open-ended urban project capable of evolving without losing its initial character. Heritage preservation was the backdrop and the new buildings were governed by it, in an ongoing dialogue with their setting. Public space was the overall linking factor in a project that took shape step by step. In our role as coordinators we ran the themed workshops that brought together the architects for the different batches for two years of full-time research into definition of common design rules. Little by little the tentative approaches of the beginning developed into something self-evident: the barracks opened up to the neighbourhood with no loss of its original identity.

La transformation de cette ancienne caserne devait être exemplaire, dans le respect du contexte et dans l'échange avec l'ensemble des publics concernés. Nous avons mis en place une stratégie douce, un principe de projet urbain ouvert, capable d'évoluer sans perdre son caractère premier. Le patrimoine conservé forme le fond de scène du projet ; les nouvelles constructions s'y adossent et dialoguent avec leur contexte. L'espace public fait le lien entre tous ces éléments. Le projet s'est mis en place pas à pas. En tant que coordinateurs, nous avons géré les ateliers thématiques qui ont réuni durant deux ans les architectes des différents lots pour définir les règles communes de conception, dans une recherche permanente. Les premiers tâtonnements se sont progressivement transformés en évidences. La caserne s'est ouverte au quartier, sans perdre son identité originelle.

Public spaces of the Reuilly barracks, Paris

ESPACE LIBRE
DE CONVIVIABILITE
NOUE HUMIDE

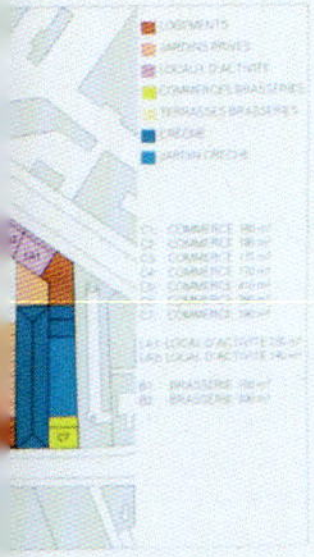

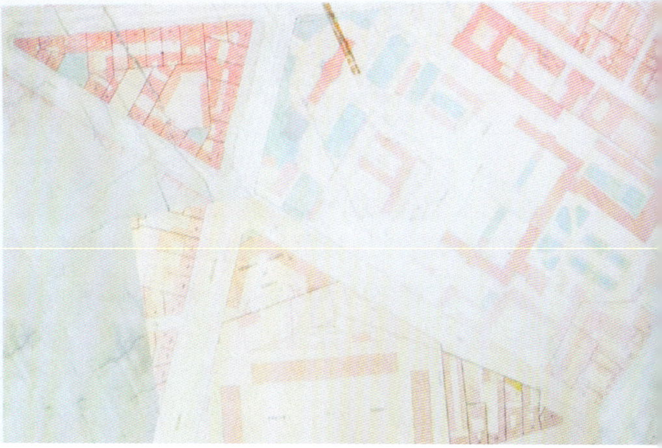

The former parade ground at the Reuilly barracks formed a central void, a breathing space at the heart of the site. Having chosen to preserve it as such, we densified the buildings around it and turned its stoniness into a garden offering a winding path from Boulevard Diderot to Rue de Reuilly and Rue de Chaligny. The fencing of the garden is discreetly integrated into shallow ditches planted out to maintain visual continuity and give the impression that the green space also embraces the foot of the buildings. A garden in Paris must be universally welcoming, provide the expected uses and invent new ones. In consultation with local residents and taking biodiversity into account, a multifaceted programme has been implemented, including a wetland, gardens for immersion in flowers and fragrances, games for children, individual and collective seating, a fountain, etc. A principle of playful undulation orchestrates the site, with its ups and downs hosting different activities in different ambiences. Trees that have been retained, together with newly introduced species, are dotted around a site fashioned by its natural pathways.

L'ancienne place d'armes de la caserne de Reuilly forme un vide central, une respiration au cœur du site. Nous avons densifié les bâtiments qui l'entourent et choisi de préserver ce vide. La place, minérale, a été transformée en jardin, permettant la traversée de passage à passage entre le boulevard Diderot et les rues de Reuilly et de Chaligny. Les clôtures du jardin sont intégrées en creux, dans des noues plantées, afin de ménager une continuité visuelle et de donner l'impression que l'espace végétal englobe également les pieds des bâtiments. Un jardin dans Paris doit pouvoir accueillir tous les publics, proposer les usages attendus, en inventer d'autres. En concertation avec les riverains et dans le respect de la biodiversité, une programmation multiple a été mise en place avec un milieu humide, des jardins immersifs de fleurs et de parfums, des jeux pour enfants, des assises simples ou collectives, une fontaine, etc. Un principe d'ondulations ludiques organise les lieux, les usages prenant place sur les reliefs successifs, qui offrent différentes ambiances. Arbres conservés et nouvelles essences ponctuent l'espace, mis en forme par les cheminements naturels.

 Public spaces of the Reuilly barracks, Paris

Built in 1878, the Palais du Trocadéro was radically modified to make room for the Palais de Chaillot at the 1937 World's Fair. It is now home to a number of institutions, among them the National Maritime Museum, in the west wing. The 1937 project doubled the size of the 1878 building with exterior and interior additions that increased its exhibition area and provided a new image more in tune with the times. Our project draws on this revamped structure and its two long, continuous spaces. Visitor itineraries have been reinvented so as to create a loop running from the entrance and its mysterious ambience to the end pavilion, newly reopened onto the city and revealed in all its vertical splendour. The new programmes bear on the mezzanines, whose enveloping shape brings to light the "streamlined" spaces of the galleries. The outcome is new areas that seem to have been created by subtraction rather than addition. The thickness of the envelope makes it a functional separation that frees the exhibition spaces from technical constraints. The smoothness of the trajectories is further enhanced by the sinuous floor markings that greet the visitor on arrival. This is architecture scaled to the human body and taking shape within an envelope at once harmonious and continuous.

Le palais du Trocadéro, construit en 1878, fut lourdement transformé pour laisser place au palais de Chaillot lors de l'Exposition internationale de 1937. Il accueille aujourd'hui plusieurs établissements, notamment le musée de la Marine dans l'aile ouest. Le projet de 1937 a doublé la structure du palais de 1878 par l'ajout d'épaisseurs extérieure et intérieure, offrant davantage de surface ainsi qu'une nouvelle image plus en adéquation avec son temps. Notre projet s'appuie sur cette architecture revêtue qui dessine deux longs espaces continus. Les parcours ont été réinventés en vue de créer une boucle de visite, depuis l'entrée, à l'atmosphère mystérieuse, jusqu'au pavillon d'about réouvert sur la ville et révélé dans sa verticalité. Les nouveaux programmes prennent place dans des mezzanines dont le dessin enveloppant révèle les espaces « carrossés » des galeries. Ainsi les surfaces ajoutées semblent-elles créées par soustraction plutôt que par addition. L'épaisseur de l'enveloppe devient un entre-deux fonctionnel, permettant de libérer les espaces d'exposition des contraintes techniques. La fluidité des trajectoires est confortée par le marquage sinueux du sol qui vient chercher le visiteur à l'entrée. L'architecture se met à l'échelle du corps, prenant forme dans une enveloppe harmonieuse et continue.

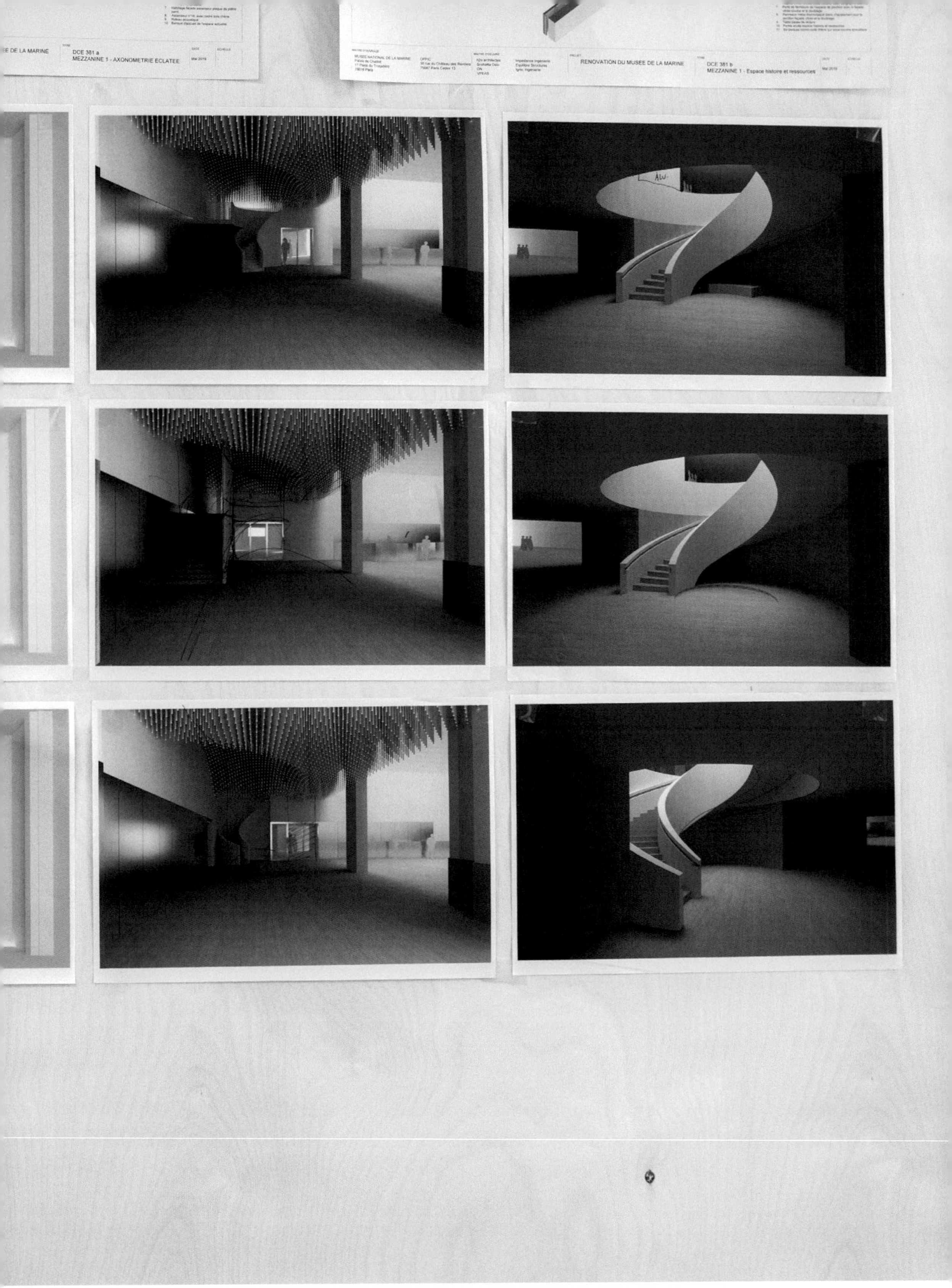
DCE 381 a
MEZZANINE 1 - AXONOMETRIE ECLATEE
RENOVATION DU MUSEE DE LA MARINE
DCE 381 b
MEZZANINE 1 - Espace histoire et ressources

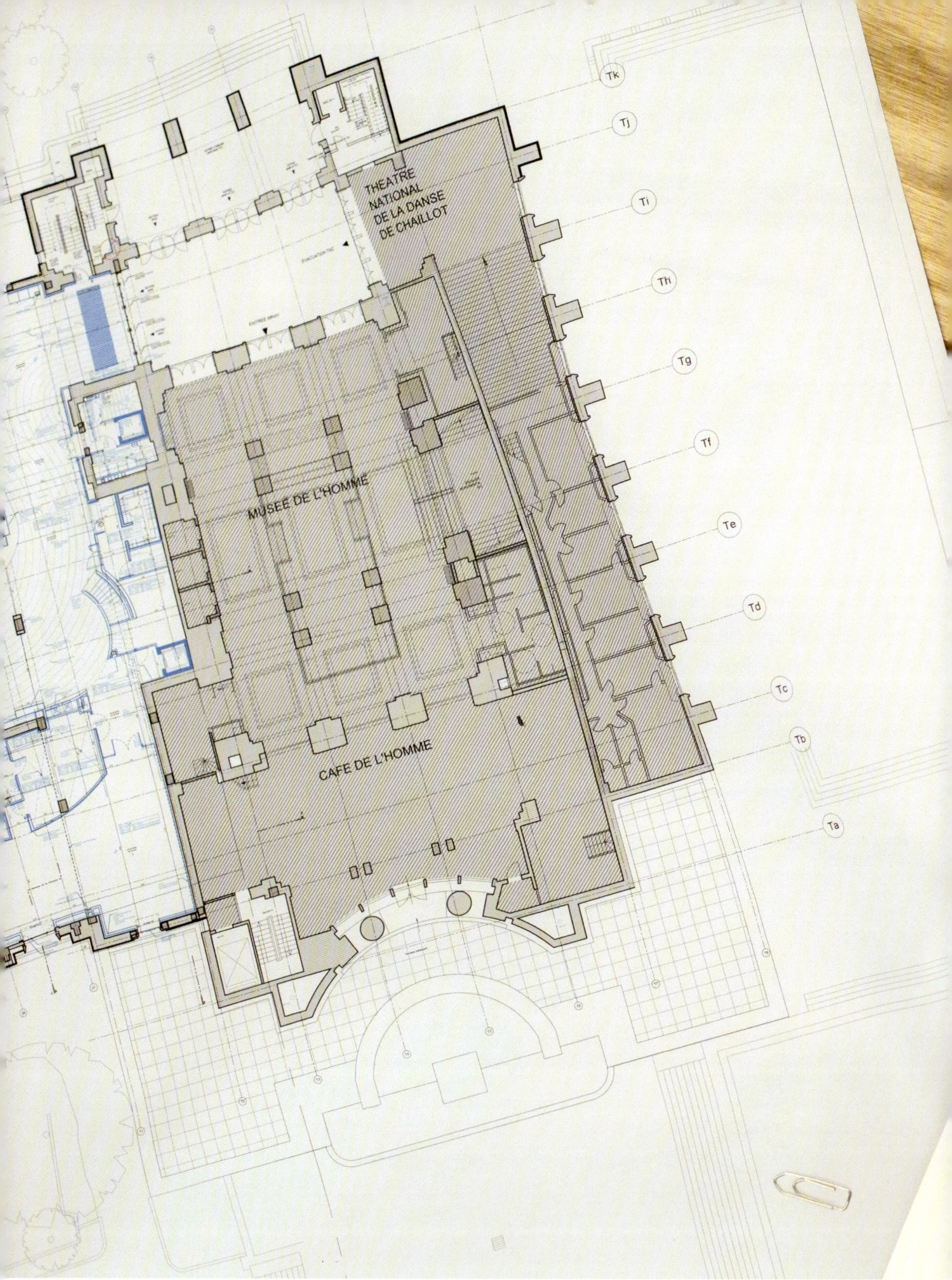
THEATRE NATIONAL DE LA DANSE DE CHAILLOT
MUSEE DE L'HOMME
CAFE DE L'HOMME
Tk
Tj
Ti
Th
Tg
Tf
Te
Td
Tc
Tb
Ta

Musée national
de la Marine

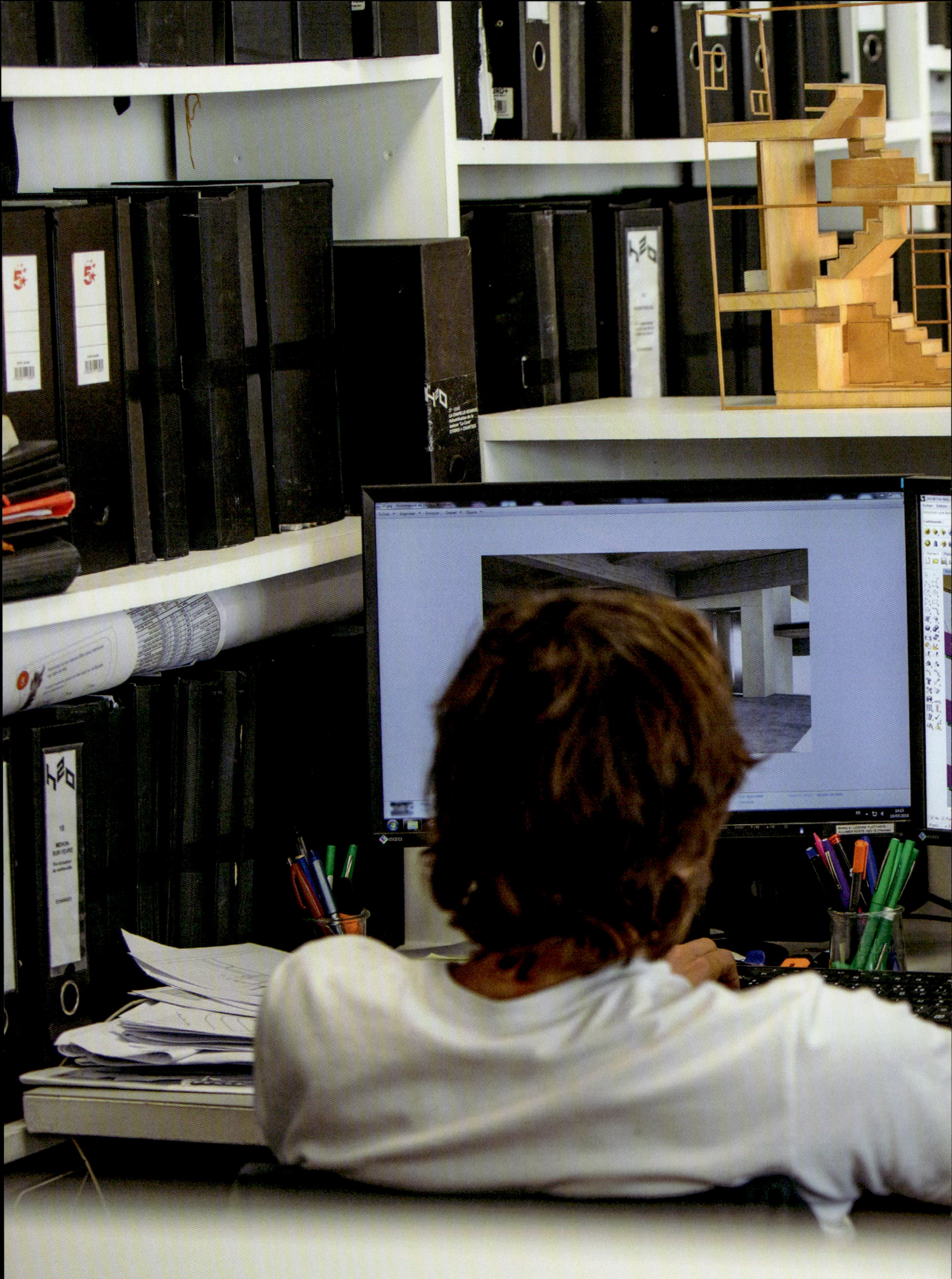

 Office building, Villa du Clos de Malevart, Paris

h2o

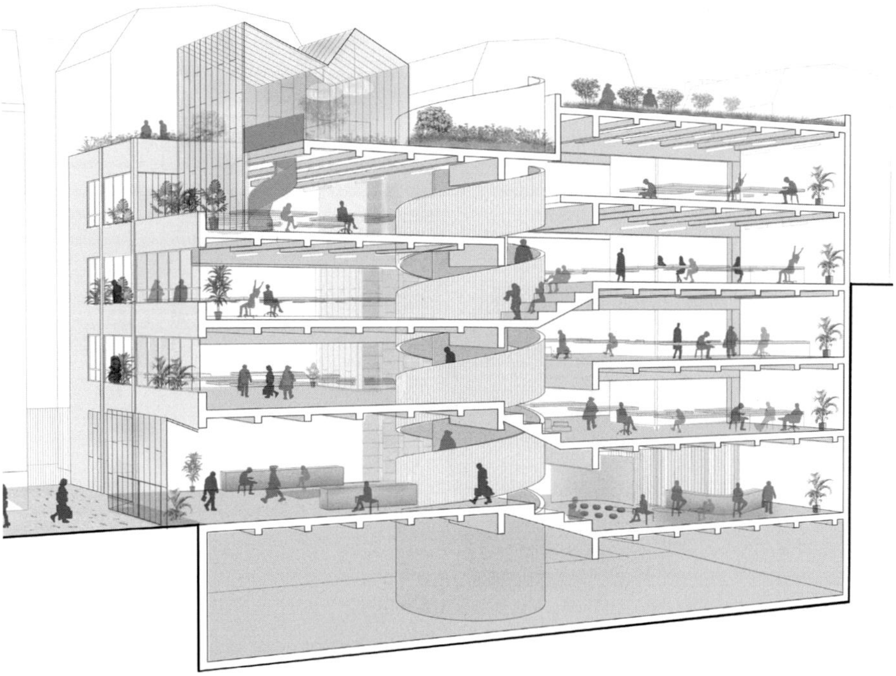

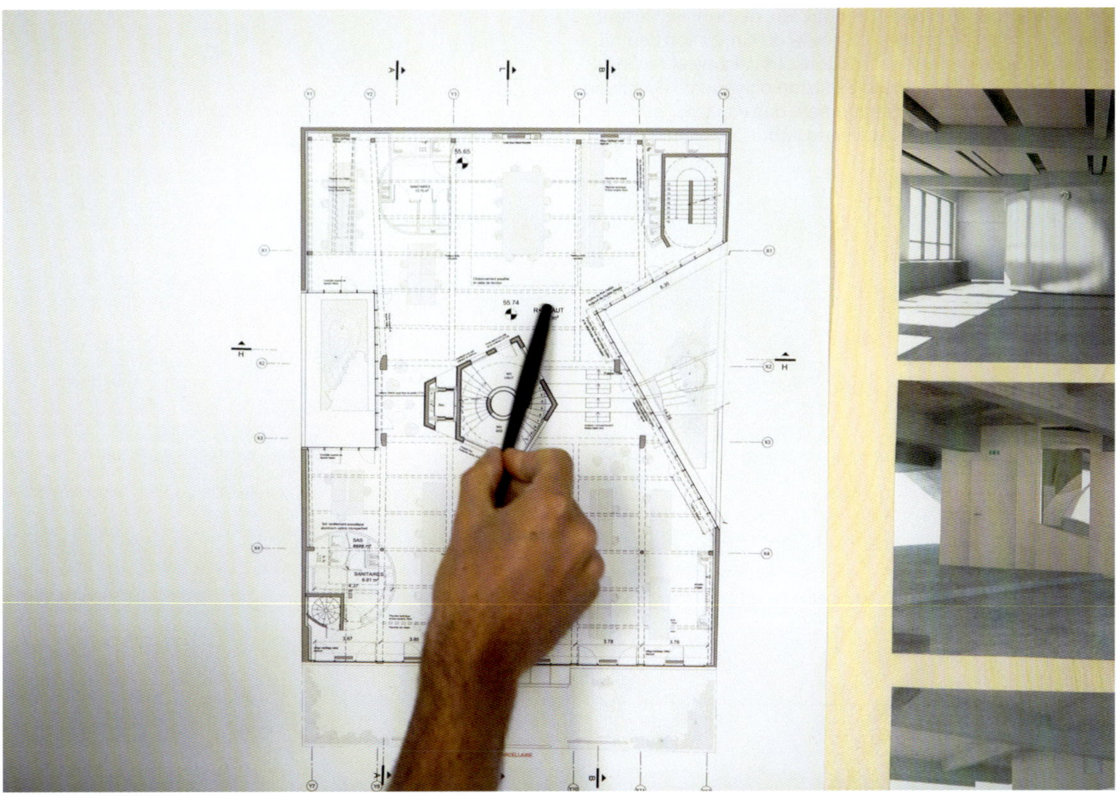

The programme consisted in making an office block out of a former parking garage set deep in a city block at the end of the Villa du Clos de Malevart cul-de-sac. In this monobloc building with three blind, regular, composite facades, the half-levels were connected by continuous ramps. We reprogrammed this space by drawing on the virtues of the existing building. In addition to the heritage conservation issues, it was a question of saving the energy that would have been required for the demolition, which was too complex given the dead-end situation. We therefore retained as many original elements as possible, and rebuilt on the basis of the initial volume, breaking the structure up with courtyards to bring in more light and open up views. Continuous and ascending, the space revolves around a central core, while the half-levels are linked by sets of steps The generously proportioned central circulation core duplicates these connections and encourages encounters between users. Its polygonal shape makes the routes more dynamic and influenced the layout of the spaces. The roof has been planted out as a communal garden.

Le programme consistait à reconvertir en bureaux un ancien parking implanté en cœur d'îlot, au fond d'une impasse composée, la villa du Clos de Malevart. Dans ce bâtiment monobloc doté de trois façades aveugles, régulières et composées, les étages en demi-niveaux sont reliés par des rampes continues. Nous avons reprogrammé cet espace tout en nous appuyant sur les qualités de l'existant. Au-delà des enjeux patrimoniaux de conservation, il s'agissait en effet d'économiser l'énergie qu'aurait nécessitée la démolition, trop complexe étant donné la situation en fond d'impasse. Nous avons donc conservé un maximum d'éléments, et reconstruit l'architecture à partir de son volume initial en le découpant de cours, afin de laisser entrer la lumière et de dégager des vues. L'espace, continu et ascendant, s'enroule autour d'un noyau central. Les demi-niveaux sont reliés par un jeu de gradins. Le noyau de circulation central, aux dimensions généreuses, double ces liaisons et favorise les rencontres entre usagers. Sa forme polygonale dynamise les parcours et induit l'aménagement des espaces. La toiture, végétalisée, est devenue jardin commun.

Light and dismountable, the MUE pavilion can be moved on demand in the vicinity of the universities of Burgundy and Franche-Comté, in response to a variety of audiences. Its open-arms shape conveys its welcoming aspect and its sliding doors allow for interaction with its context, especially in good weather. Its modular construction is based on wooden boxes: these had to be transported by hand, a determining factor in their size and weight. Once assembled, the components form a shell that provides the necessary rigidity, in the manner of an aeroplane wing. The roof and facade are cladded with aluminium to make them waterproof. Inside, wood bent and stretched ensures a comfortable ambience.

Démontable et léger, le pavillon MUE se déplace au gré des demandes, dans les environs des universités de Bourgogne et de Franche-Comté, pour aller au-devant de publics variés. Sa forme évoquant des bras ouverts donne à lire sa fonction d'accueil, la mobilité de ses ouvertures lui permet d'interagir avec son contexte, notamment aux beaux jours. La construction, modulaire, est composée de caissons en bois transportables à la main, ce qui a conditionné leurs dimensions et leur poids. Une fois assemblés, les éléments forment une coque qui donne une rigidité suffisante au pavillon, à la manière d'une aile d'avion. Cette coque est revêtue d'aluminium en couverture et en façade, pour assurer l'étanchéité. À l'intérieur, le bois courbé et tendu dispense une atmosphère confortable.

AXTON

Spaces: rhumbs
Frédéric Forte

Frédéric Forte was born in Toulouse in 1973 and now lives in Paris. A poet, he has been a member of the Oulipo group of experimental writers since 2005. His initials are those of the "fixed forms" whose potentialities he enjoys exploring, either as elements of poetic traditions or more recent Oulipian creations. He is the inventor of the poetic forms instant opera, elementary mobile morale, bristols, 99 preliminary notes and the rhumbs illustrated in the following pages. No gambit is unacceptable to him – not even prose or free verse. He has recently published *Dire ouf* (P.O.L, 2016), *Été 18* (L'Usage, 2020) and *Nous allons perdre deux minutes de lumière* (P.O.L, 2020).

Frédéric Forte's rhumb is a poetic form its inventor has been honing since 2014. In sea-going terminology a rhumb is the angular space formed by the segments of a 32-wind compass rose. Taking as his starting point the concept of site-specific writing, Forte places himself "at the centre of a compass rose, recounting his surroundings in lines of verse extending outwards toward the eight main points of the compass" and rotating around a fixed point. The length of each line is determined by the depth of field available to the writer. This is a spatial constraint transcribed onto the territory of paper: the further away the vanishing point, the longer the line of verse. Impressed by Forte's work, h2o asked him to devote five rhumbs to projects typical of their urban development approach. This led the poet to the Familistère at Guise, the cathedral in Évreux, the Reuilly barracks site and the main courtyard of the National Assembly in Paris, scrupulously noting the relevant geographical coordinates each time. In lines embracing sounds, sensations, ideas and observations, Forte offers the imagination a subtle, situated vision of these different places.

The English rendering of Frédéric Forte's rhumbs is the work of poet and translator Michelle Noteboom.

some live fire in the landscape/a sign
crossing the h2o to the mausoleum
the Oise below and the whole world happening
beneath the dome the workers make us new with the old
right there in the corner: the extremely accurate form of utopia
tensing toward the tender, bowing green homes, horizon-line forest
a runway strip fashioned from ordinary planks: tops of trees, hello heavens
walking the boardwalks a few centimetres up above (thank you) the idea of nature

Monsieur Godin beckoning at the Palace invites us

under the umbrella, left wing new skin

benches punctuating, detailed red bricks

a theater for all

public school where we learn/point the angle

toward another patch of the city same and different

all windows familiar to the collective body

blue anorak (living there)

module Alpha at the western gate

sandwich-break on the parvis

along the guardrails (the river's there) toward the old Printemps

watch out: garage exit

a little girl cluck-clucks at the top of her lungs to a backdrop of deaf

a line of windows with a view of the lion, its matchbox palace

and cash! the postman quick

on rippled mineral sheet, the map of cobblestones peppered with twigs, steps/palimpsest

worker commotion, pandemonium at play, labeled apartments

in which direction can we actually be looking?

tumulus and old tree make an archeo-decor

underfoot, yellow draws the paving design

on the passage side is the city: a bush rubs elbows with the clouds

planter box of flagstone-prototypes

through the frame we see, cable-wires, the inside

oh a dohyō soil in one hell of a state

gently sloped shapes launch an attack on the hemicycle

and equipment (piled up in a yellow dumpster)

heels clicking through the diagonal

the rhythm of the court all in supports/surfaces

crossing, from one bollard to another, the flags and gate: hello there Republic!

here, the world phones or smokes

serviceberry, Japanese air

cigarette, she thinks, back to the wall

Espaces : rhumbs
Frédéric Forte

Frédéric Forte est né à Toulouse en 1973 et vit à Paris. Il est poète et membre de l'Oulipo depuis 2005. Ses initiales sont celles de « formes fixes » dont il aime explorer les potentialités, qu'elles soient issues des traditions poétiques ou conçues plus récemment par les oulipiens. Il est l'inventeur des formes poétiques de l'opéra-minute, de la petite morale élémentaire portative, des bristols, des 99 notes préparatoires ou encore des rhumbs illustrés ci-après. Il ne s'interdit aucune voie, pas même la prose ou le vers libre. Il a publié récemment *Dire ouf* (P.O.L, 2016), *Été 18* (L'Usage, 2020) et *Nous allons perdre deux minutes de lumière* (P.O.L, 2020).

Le rhumb est une forme poétique développée par Frédéric Forte depuis 2014. Dans le vocabulaire de la marine, un rhumb désigne l'espace angulaire séparant les trente-deux aires de vent de la boussole. Selon un principe d'écriture *in situ*, le poète se place « au centre d'une rose des vents pour dire son environnement en composant des vers qui regardent dans les huit directions principales » à partir d'une rotation autour d'un point fixe. La longueur des lignes est délimitée par la profondeur du champ visuel ouvert devant l'auteur. Cette contrainte spatiale se transcrit sur le territoire du papier : plus le point de fuite est éloigné, plus le vers sera long. Sensible au travail de Forte, h2o lui a proposé d'écrire cinq rhumbs sur les lieux représentatifs de leurs projets d'aménagement urbain. Le poète s'est ainsi rendu au familistère de Guise, à la cathédrale d'Évreux, sur le chantier de la caserne de Reuilly et dans la cour d'honneur de l'Assemblée nationale à Paris, notant précisément ses coordonnées de localisation. Consignant dans ses vers sons, sensations, pensées et observations, le poète donne à imaginer ces lieux selon une lecture sensible et située.

La version anglaise des rhumbs a été assurée par la poète et traductrice Michelle Noteboom.

du feu vif dans le paysage/un signe

qui franchit l'h2o vers le mausolée

l'Oise en dessous et tout le monde déroulant

sous la coupole les ouvriers nous font du neuf avec du vieux

juste dans la lucarne là, au but : la forme très précise de l'utopie

tendue vers le vert tendre, boulodrome maisons, ligne sylvestre-horizon

une piste d'envol faite de planches ordinaires : cime des arbres, hello le ciel

parcourant les pontons quelques centimètres au-dessus (merci !) de la nature idéale

Monsieur Godin main tendue au Palais nous invite

sous le parapluie, l'aile gauche peau neuve

bancs qui virgulent, briques rouges au détail

un théâtre pour tous

école publique où apprendre/flécher l'angle

vers un autre morceau de la ville même et différent

toutes fenêtres familières au corps collectif

anorak bleu (y habitant)

et cash ! le facteur vite

sur nappe ondulant minérale, la carte des pavés relevés de brindilles, de pas/palimpseste

module Alpha au portail ouest

pause-sandwich sur le parvis

le long du garde-corps (la rive est là) vers le vieux Printemps

attention ! sortie de garage

une petite fille cot-cot-codète à tue-tête sur fond d'enseigne *SURDITÉ*

enfilées les fenêtres avec vue sur l'Iton, son palais d'allumettes

foisonnement ouvrier, jeu de brouillages, appartements étiquetés

dans quelle direction regarde-t-on vraiment ?

tumulus et arbre vieux font un archéo-décor

au sol, tracé jaune, le dessin du pavage

du côté du passage il y a la ville : un arbuste haut tutoie les nuages

jardinière de pavés-prototypes

par le cadre on perçoit, branchements, l'intérieur

oh un dohyō ! terre dans tous ses états

formes en pente douce partent à l'assaut de l'hémicycle

et du matériel (entassé dans une benne jaune)

talons qui claquent dans la diagonale

le rythme de la cour tout en supports/surfaces

franchissant, d'un potelet à l'autre, les drapeaux et la grille : salut, la République !

ici, le monde phone ou fume

amélancier, air japonais

cigarette, pense-t-elle, dos au mur

A fable Bernard Tschumi

Bernard Tschumi (born 1944) is a professor at the Graduate School of Architecture, Planning and Preservation at Columbia University in New York, where he was Dean from 1988 to 2003. He lives and works in Paris and New York, with an architectural office in each city. After graduating from the Swiss Federal Institute of Technology in Zurich, he devoted some fifteen years to teaching and research. His books include *The Manhattan Transcripts* and *Architecture and Disjunction*, among others. Since winning the international competition for the Parc de la Villette in Paris in 1983, he has completed a wide range of projects, including Le Fresnoy (the National Studio for Contemporary Arts) in Tourcoing, France; the Acropolis Museum in Athens; the Zenith concert halls in Limoges and Rouen; the headquarters for Vacheron Constantin in Geneva; the school of architecture for Florida International University in Miami; and the new architecture for the renovated Parc Zoologique de Paris, among others. In 1996 Tschumi was awarded France's Grand Prix National d'Architecture. Two major retrospectives – at The Museum of Modern Art in New York (1994) and the Centre Georges Pompidou in Paris (2014) – have paid tribute to his built and theoretical work.

Sometimes it's useful to plunge into the past so as to understand the present and even anticipate the future. In a well-known book dating from the 1970s, the historian and critic Colin Rowe posits two distinct approaches in the history of ideas and architecture[1]. The first is the single "big idea", which serves as a line of conduct for all human endeavors. The second, more nuanced, can accommodate several ideas simultaneously and does not seek coherence at all costs.

Rowe opposes the hedgehog, representing the big idea, to the fox, representing multiplicity. In the hedgehog family are such greats of the Modern Movement as Gropius and Mies, while the fox family is made up of remarkable individual talents like Aalto and Asplund. This dichotomy has left its stamp on many of the ideologies that have shaped the history of architecture throughout the ages.

In any consideration of the architectural movements, large and small, of the second half of the twentieth century, it's tempting to make comparisons with the fabled fox and hedgehog: think of architecture that is "rational", "radical", "neo-modern", "postmodern", "historicist", "regionalist", "minimalist", "deconstructivist", "digital", "ecological", or "neo-figurative".

The overriding question, however, may be how to situate architecture in this early part of the twenty-first century. Is there a dominant trend, an architectural establishment developing independent of those twentieth-century eminences, some of them still among us? Who, today, wields power or influence (which are not the same thing)? Given the looming importance of the issue of climate change, there is a real temptation to paraphrase a famous writer of the past and declare, "The twenty-first century will be 'green' or it will not be."[2]

The real situation is without doubt more nuanced. Among the young offices currently contributing to architectural history, it is interesting to consider the work of Paris-based h2o, some ten years old at this writing. The particularity of the approach of this team is its frequent focus on an existing problem requiring a site-specific solution. No trumpeting of grand ideological strategies here: the method is, above all, tactical. As h2o puts it, the task is to "engage in a subtle dialogue with the context"; "We're grafting, and the graft has to take root."

Whatever the scale of their projects, from the imposing Familistère at Guise to La Cabotte, a small pavilion set amid vineyards, "the starting point is right now, everything has to move fast." As the team members insist, "It's not abstract ideas that are up for debate, but rather the here and the now." Rather than starting from a story to make a place, it's about making a place that suggests a story. All of which brings us back to our fable of the fox and the hedgehog. Might h2o's architects typically be smart, talented foxes, making the most of the specificity of the multiple contexts in which they work?

Is it really that simple? Rejecting all dogmatism, h2o is forging its own history out of a radicality imbued with restraint. "Open-ended" but sufficiently structured to evolve, their project involves strategy every step of the way. This clarity of intention also sets h2o among the hedgehogs. And this duality makes the office a prime example of the world we live in, of a new practice of architecture that starts out from existing circumstances in order to address far larger environmental issues.

1 See Colin Rowe and Fred Koetter, *Collage City* (Cambridge, MA/London: MIT Press, 1978) and Isaiah Berlin, *The Hedgehog and the Fox* (London: Weidenfeld and Nicolson, 1951).

2 "The twenty-first century will be religious [*or* spiritual, *or* mystical] or it will not be." The original statement is attributed, rightly or wrongly, to André Malraux.

Fable
Bernard Tschumi

Bernard Tschumi (né en 1944) est architecte et professeur à la Graduate School of Architecture, Planning and Preservation de l'université Columbia (New York), dont il a été le doyen de 1988 à 2003. Il vit et travaille entre Paris et New York, où il a fondé ses deux agences. Après des études à l'École polytechnique fédérale de Zurich, il se consacre durant près de quinze ans à l'enseignement et à la recherche, publiant des ouvrages parmi lesquels *The Manhattan Transcripts* et *Architecture and Disjunction*. Lauréat du concours international du parc de la Villette (Paris) en 1983, l'architecte réalise ensuite des projets variés comme l'école d'art du Fresnoy (Tourcoing), le musée de l'Acropole (Athènes), les Zénith de Limoges et Rouen, le siège de Vacheron Constantin (Genève), l'école d'architecture de l'université de Floride (Miami) ou encore le parc zoologique de Paris. Bernard Tschumi a reçu en 1996 le Grand Prix national d'architecture tandis que deux importantes rétrospectives au MoMA (New York, 1994) et au Centre Pompidou (Paris, 2014) ont salué son œuvre construite comme théorique.

Il est parfois utile de se plonger dans le passé pour comprendre le présent, et peut-être pour anticiper le futur. Dans un texte resté fameux, écrit dans les années 1970, l'historien et critique Colin Rowe propose deux positions distinctes dans l'histoire de la pensée et celle de l'architecture[1]. La première est celle de la grande idée dominante (*big idea*) et sert de ligne de conduite sur tous les projets de l'existence. La deuxième est plus nuancée, elle peut accueillir plusieurs idées simultanément et ne recherche pas la cohérence à tout prix.

Rowe oppose ainsi *the hedgehog* (le hérisson), représentant la grande idée, et *the fox* (le renard), représentant la multiplicité. Dans la famille des hérissons, on trouve les grandes figures du Mouvement moderne (Gropius, Mies, etc.). Dans celle des renards, on trouve d'exceptionnels architectes de talent (Aalto, Asplund, etc.). L'opposition de ces deux approches est caractéristique de beaucoup d'idéologies qui ont fait l'histoire de l'architecture à travers les temps.

Ainsi, il est tentant d'observer les grands et petits mouvements de l'architecture de la deuxième moitié du XXe siècle en les comparant au renard et au hérisson de la fable. Pensez architecture « rationnelle », « radicale », « néo-moderne », « postmoderne », « historiciste », « régionaliste », « minimaliste », « déconstructiviste », « numérique », « écologique » ou « néo-figurative ».

On peut surtout se poser la question de comment situer l'architecture au début du XXIe siècle. Y a-t-il une tendance dominante : un *establishment* architectural en formation, indépendamment des grandes figures du XXe siècle, certaines encore présentes ? Qui, aujourd'hui, a le pouvoir ou a de l'influence (ce qui n'est pas la même chose) ? Au vu de l'importance prise par la question du réchauffement climatique au début du nouveau siècle, la tentation est grande de paraphraser un auteur célèbre et d'annoncer : « Le XXIe siècle sera “vert” ou ne sera pas[2]. »

La réalité est sans doute plus nuancée. Parmi les jeunes agences qui font partie de l'histoire aujourd'hui, il est intéressant de regarder le travail de l'équipe de h2o, basée à Paris, en existence depuis une dizaine d'années au moment où s'écrivent ces lignes. Les recherches de cette équipe ont pour particularité de presque toujours partir d'un problème existant à résoudre sur le terrain. Plutôt que de clamer de grandes stratégies idéologiques, l'approche est avant tout tactique. Comme h2o l'exprime, il faut « assumer un dialogue fin avec le contexte » ; « on fait une greffe, il faut que cela prenne ».

Quelle que soit l'échelle de leurs projets, de la réhabilitation du familistère de Guise à La Cabotte, petit pavillon au milieu des vignes, « le point de départ est dans l'immédiat, tout doit aller vite ». Comme le soulignent les membres de l'équipe, « ce ne sont pas les idées abstraites qui font le débat, mais c'est ici et maintenant ». Plutôt que de partir d'une histoire pour faire un lieu, il s'agit de faire un lieu qui propose une histoire. Cela nous ramène à notre fable du renard et du hérisson. Les architectes d'h2o seraient-ils donc typiquement des renards futés et talentueux, tirant avantage de la spécificité des multiples contextes dans lesquels ils travaillent ?

Mais est-ce si simple? En refusant tout dogmatisme, h2o se forge une histoire à travers une radicalité tout en retenue. Leur « projet ouvert », suffisamment structuré pour évoluer, c'est de la stratégie à toutes les phases. En cela, la clarté du propos de h2o fait qu'ils appartiennent aussi au monde des hérissons. Dans cette dualité, h2o est exemplaire du monde où nous vivons, d'une nouvelle pratique de l'architecture, qui part de l'existant pour tenter de répondre à de vastes enjeux environnementaux.

1 Voir Colin Rowe et Fred Koetter, *Collage City* (1978), ainsi que Isaiah Berlin, *The Hedgehog and the Fox* (1951).
2 « Le XXIe siècle sera religieux [ou spirituel, ou mystique] ou ne sera pas », citation attribuée à tort ou à raison à André Malraux (1975).

350 Index

Index

Year **Année**	*Title* **Titre**	*Programme* **Programme**	*Location* **Lieu**	*Floor area* **Surface**	*Type* **Statut**	*Client* **Maîtrise d'ouvrage**
2000	*Ciba warehouse* Entrepôt Ciba	*Construction of a warehouse with offices* Construction d'un entrepôt commercial avec bureaux	*Châteaubriant (44), France*	*1,028 m²* 1 028 m²	*Completed* Réalisé	*Ciba Ouary*
2002	*Cigex storage* Stockage Cigex	*Extension to a storage building* Agrandissement d'un bâtiment de stockage	*Candé (49), France*	*1,200 m²* 1 200 m²	*Completed* Réalisé	*Cigex*
2002	*Architecture for Humanity mobile clinic* Clinique mobile Architecture for Humanity	*Construction of a mobile clinic for AIDS patients* Construction d'une clinique mobile pour malades du SIDA	*Sub-Saharan Africa* Afrique sub-saharienne	*100 m²*	*Competition* Concours	*Architecture for Humanity (AFH)*
2003	*Cigex office* Bureau Cigex	*Creation of an executive office* Création d'un bureau de direction	*Candé (49), France*	–	*Completed* Réalisé	*Cigex*
2003	*Cigex showroom* Comptoir Cigex	*Reconfiguration of the entrance and creation of sales counters* Réaménagement de l'accueil du magasin et création de comptoirs de vente	*Candé (49), France*	–	*Completed* Réalisé	*Ciba Ouary*
2004	*Panik*	*Design of a micro-space for stress relief* Conception d'un micro-espace de décompression du stress	*Brussels, Belgium* Bruxelles, Belgique	*3 m²*	*Completed* Réalisé	*Panik*
2005	*Parade ground* Place d'armes	*Landscaping of the parade ground with a fountain and design of a collection of urban furniture* Aménagement urbain de la place d'armes avec fontaine et conception d'une ligne de mobilier urbain	*Valenciennes (59), France*	*1,262 m²* 1 262 m²	*On hold* Suspendu	*City of Valenciennes* Ville de Valenciennes
2006	*Modular bench* Banc modulaire	*Design of a collection of urban seats and benches* Conception d'une ligne de fauteuils et de bancs urbains	–	–	*Completed* Réalisé	*Developed with Lafarge, distributed by Azuly* Développé avec Lafarge, distribué par Azuly
		Team: Nicolas Sterling (structure engineer), Miguel Mazeri (anthropologist) Équipe : Nicolas Sterling (ingénierie structure), Miguel Mazeri (anthropologue)				
		p. 42				
2006	*La Colline houses* Maisons La Colline	*Construction of 4 individual houses within a landscape redesign* Construction de 4 maisons individuelles au sein d'un aménagement paysager	*Tameslohte, Morocco* Tameslohte, Maroc	*920 m² × 4*	*On hold* Suspendu	*La Constancia*
		Team: J. Cadilhac (architect), Associati (architect of record) Équipe : J. Cadilhac (architecte), Associati (architecte local)				
		p. 32				
2006	*Habitable pavilion* Pavillon d'habitation	*Transformation of a garden pavilion into a teenager's living quarters* Réaménagement d'un pavillon de jardin en habitat pour adolescent	*Chatou (78), France*	*24 m²*	*Completed* Réalisé	*Private* Privée
		p. 228				
2006	*Seven Hotel*	*Construction of a 100-room hotel with associated services* Construction d'un hôtel de 100 chambres avec services associés	*Bangalore, India* Bangalore, Inde	*4,500 m²* 4 500 m²	*On hold* Suspendu	*Bang/Seven Hotels*
2007	*Bénédictine Palace* Palais Bénédictine	*Redesign of the main courtyard* Aménagement de la cour d'honneur	*Fécamp (76), France*	*300 m²*	*On hold* Suspendu	*Bacardi*
2007	*Business incubator* Pépinière d'entreprises	*Rehabilitation of a former packaging factory as a business incubator and training centre* Réhabilitation d'une ancienne cartonnerie en pépinière d'entreprises et centre de formation	*Pont-Audemer (27), France*	*1,500 m²* 1 500 m²	*Completed* Réalisé	*EPF Normandie, Pont-Audemer Intermunicipal Community* EPF Normandie, Communauté de communes de Pont-Audemer
		Team: Ingénierie Louis Choulet (mechanical and sustainability engineer), France Aires (exterior infrastructure engineer), Cabinet Virtz (quantity surveyor) Équipe : Ingénierie Louis Choulet (ingénierie fluides et HQE), France Aires (ingénierie VRD), Cabinet Virtz (économiste)				
		p. 194				
2008	*Surroundings of the cathedral* Abords de la cathédrale	*Reconfiguration of the public space* Reconfiguration de l'espace public	*Évreux (27), France*	*4 ha*	*Completed* Réalisé	*City of Évreux* Ville d'Évreux
		Team: Michel Desvigne paysagiste (landscape representative), France Aires (exterior infrastructure engineer) Équipe : Michel Desvigne paysagiste (mandataire), France Aires (ingénierie VRD)				
		p. 258				
2008	*Front and Back apartment* Appartement recto-verso	*Transformation of an apartment* Réaménagement d'un appartement	*Paris (75010), France*	*60 m²*	*Completed* Réalisé	*Private* Privée

2008	*Dewailly cloister* Cloître Dewailly	*Transformation of a cloister into a cultural space* Réaménagement d'un cloître en espace culturel	*Amiens (80), France*	*800 m²*	*Competition* Concours	*City of Amiens* Ville d'Amiens
2008	*Cavaignac building* Immeuble Cavaignac	*Rehabilitation and extension of 20 apartments and 3 retail spaces on Rue Godefroy-Cavaignac* Réhabilitation et extension d'un immeuble de 20 logements et 3 locaux commerciaux rue Godefroy-Cavaignac	*Paris (75011), France*	*1,850 m²* 1 850 m²	*Completed* Réalisé	*SIEMP*
2009	*Coligny Hotel* Hôtel Coligny	*Construction of a luxury hotel and wellness centre* Construction d'un centre hôtelier de luxe et centre de soins	*Châtillon-Coligny (45), France*	*6,000 m²* 6 000 m²	*On hold* Suspendu	*Ylang Investissements hôteliers*
2009	*Eva's bed* Lit d'Eva	*Redesign of a child's room* Aménagement d'une chambre d'enfant	*Paris (75010), France*	*9 m²*	*Completed* Réalisé	*Private* Privée
2009	*House B* Maison B	*Construction of an individual house* Construction d'une maison individuelle	*Puteaux (92), France*	*120 m²*	*On hold* Suspendu	*Private* Privée
2009	*Wallpaper* house* Maison Wallpaper*	*Design of a generic individual house* Conception d'une maison individuelle générique	–	*120 m²*	*Completed* Réalisé	*Wallpaper**
		p. 54				
2009	*Grass mirror furniture* Mobilier Miroir en herbe	*Design of a mural planter* Conception d'un bac mural à végétaliser	–	–	*Completed* Réalisé	*Compagnie*
2009	*La Cabotte reception pavilion* Pavillon d'accueil La Cabotte	*Construction of a reception building, offices and wine-tasting cellar for the vineyard* Construction du bâtiment d'accueil, des bureaux et du caveau de dégustation du domaine viticole *Team: Cabinet Virtz (quantity surveyor), Nicolas Rappez (architect of record)* Équipe : Cabinet Virtz (économiste), Nicolas Rappez (architecte local)	*Mondragon (26), France*	*70 m²*	*Completed* Réalisé	*La Cabotte*
		p. 144				
2010	*Surroundings of the Familistère* Abords du familistère	*Reconfiguration of the public space: shared zone (max 20 km/h), walkways, widening of a bridge, lighting design and design of specific urban furniture* Reconfiguration de l'espace public : zone partagée (limitée à 20 km/h), passerelles, élargissement du pont, mise en lumière et conception d'un mobilier urbain spécifique *Team: Michel Desvigne paysagiste (landscape), France Aires (exterior infrastructure engineer), HDA (structure engineer)* Équipe : Michel Desvigne paysagiste, France Aires (ingénierie VRD), HDA (ingénierie structure)	*Guise (02), France*	*4 ha*	*Completed* Réalisé	*Godin Familistère Public Development Association, Aisne Department* Syndicat mixte du familistère Godin, Société d'équipement du département de l'Aisne
		p. 244				
2010	*Heart of Orly* Cœur d'Orly	*Construction of a showroom for the presentation of the new neighbourhood* Construction d'un showroom pour la présentation du nouveau quartier	*Orly (94), France*	*230 m²*	*Competition* Concours	*ADP, Covivio, Altarea Cogedim*
2010	*Folie P7*	*Rehabilitation of the Folie P7 in the Parc de la Villette for a restaurant/café* Réhabilitation de la folie P7 dans le parc de la Villette : restaurant/café	*Paris (75019), France*	*192 m²*	*Completed* Réalisé	*La Villette Public Gardens and Exhibition Hall* Établissement public du parc et de la grande halle de La Villette (EPPGHV)
2010	*Lagravère pavilions* Pavillons Lagravère	*Construction of 3 pavilions at the entrance to Parc Lagravère: reception, salespoint and restrooms* Construction de 3 pavillons d'entrée dans le parc Lagravère : accueil, point de vente, sanitaires *Team: Ingénierie Louis Choulet (mechanical and sustainability engineer), Cabinet Virtz (quantity surveyor)* Équipe : Ingénierie Louis Choulet (ingénierie fluides et HQE), Cabinet Virtz (économiste)	*Colombes (92), France*	*120 m²*	*Completed* Réalisé	*Hauts-de-Seine Department Council* Conseil général des Hauts-de-Seine
		p. 154				
2010	*French Ministry of Agriculture press room* Salle de presse du ministère de l'Agriculture	*Construction of a press room for the French Ministry of Agriculture* Construction d'une salle de presse pour le ministère de l'Agriculture	*Paris (75007), France*	*100 m²*	*Completed* Réalisé	*French Ministry of Agriculture* Ministère de l'Agriculture
2010	*MMP Milan Scenography* Scénographie MMP Milan	*Scenography for an exhibition featuring 20 designers, at the Ida Space, Zona Bovisa* Scénographie d'une exposition présentant les créations de 20 designers à l'Espace Ida, Zona Bovisa	*Milan, Italy* Milan, Italie	*140 m²*	*Completed* Réalisé	*Meet My Project*
2010	*MMP Paris Scenography* Scénographie MMP Paris	*Scenography for an exhibition featuring 20 designers in the Cité de la Création et de la Mode* Scénographie d'une exposition présentant les créations de 20 designers à la Cité de la création et de la mode	*Paris (75013), France*	*320 m²*	*Completed* Réalisé	*Meet My Project*
2011	*3 canals* 3 canaux	*Redevelopment of 3 canals in Lille's Old Town* Réaménagement urbain de 3 canaux du vieux Lille	*Lille (59), France*	*7.5 ha* 7,5 ha	*Competition* Concours	*City of Lille* Ville de Lille
2011	*Sports centre* Centre sportif	*Construction of a sports centre, with dojo and fencing room* Construction d'un centre sportif, comprenant dojo et salle d'escrime	*Beaumont-sur-Oise (95), France*	*1,730 m²* 1 730 m²	*Competition* Concours	*City of Beaumont-sur-Oise* Ville de Beaumont-sur-Oise

2011	*B5 day nursery* Crèche B5	*Construction of a day nursery for 80 children* Construction d'une crèche (80 places)	*Boulogne-Billancourt (92), France*	*1,340 m²* 1 340 m²	*Completed* Réalisé	*SAEM Val de Seine Aménagement*
2011	*Épée de Bois municipal day nursery* Crèche municipale de l'Épée de Bois	*Rehabilitation and extension of a day nursery for 24 children* Réhabilitation et extension d'une crèche (24 places) *Team: id+ ingénierie (general engineer)* Équipe : id+ ingénierie (ingénierie TCE)	*Paris (75005), France*	*300 m²*	*Completed* Réalisé	*City of Paris, DPA (Heritage and Architecture Department)* Ville de Paris, DPA (Direction du patrimoine et de l'architecture)
		p. 68				
2011	*Jeu de Paume neighbourhood amenity* Équipement de quartier Jeu de Paume	*Construction of a neighbourhood amenity: community association centre, day nursery and urban planning* Construction d'un équipement de quartier comprenant centre associatif, crèche et aménagement urbain	*Rennes (35), France*	*1,450 m²* 1 450 m²	*Competition* Concours	*City of Rennes* Ville de Rennes
2011	*Folie P5*	*Rehabilitation of the Folie workshop P5 in the Parc de la Villette for educational and leisure workshops* Réhabilitation de la folie-atelier P5 dans le parc de la Villette : ateliers pédagogiques et de loisirs	*Paris (75019), France*	*176 m²*	*Completed* Réalisé	*La Villette Public Gardens and Exhibition Hall* Établissement public du parc et de la grande halle de La Villette (EPPGHV)
2011	*Unifa building* Immeuble Unifa	*Transformation of a building into the Unifa headquarters, with exhibition spaces* Transformation d'un immeuble en siège social d'Unifa avec espaces d'exposition	*Paris (75011), France*	*2,250 m²* 2 250 m²	*Competition* Concours	*Unifa*
2011	*Tumbleweed furniture* Mobilier Tumbleweed	*Design for a garden stake* Conception d'un tuteur à végétaliser	–	–	*Completed* Réalisé	*Compagnie*
2011	*Studio des Ursulines*	*Renovation of a youth arthouse cinema (lobby and projection booth)* Rénovation d'un cinéma d'art et d'essai pour jeune public (hall d'entrée et salle de projection)	*Paris (75005), France*	*340 m²*	*Completed* Réalisé	*Studio des Ursulines*
2012	*Le Refuge apartment* Appartement Le Refuge	*Transformation of an apartment* Réaménagement d'un appartement	*Les Ménuires (73), France*	*55 m²*	*Completed* Réalisé	*Private* Privée
		p. 232				
2012	*Hypernuit offices* Bureaux Hypernuit	*Redesign of an artistic management studio's offices* Aménagement des bureaux d'un studio de direction artistique	*Paris (75018), France*	*62 m²*	*Completed* Réalisé	*Première*
2012	*Leisure centre* Centre de loisirs	*Construction of a leisure centre for children and an educational garden* Construction d'un centre multi-accueil enfants et d'un jardin pédagogique	*Ennery (95), France*	*730 m²*	*Competition* Concours	*Sausseron Valley Intermunicipal Community* Communauté de communes de la Vallée du Sausseron
2012	*Urban covered market* Halle urbaine	*Construction of an urban covered market and redesign of the Place Jean-Jaurès* Construction d'une halle urbaine et aménagement de la place Jean-Jaurès	*Limeil-Brévannes (94), France*	*4,200 m²* 4 200 m²	*Competition* Concours	*Plaine Centrale du Val-de-Marne Intermunicipal Community* Communauté d'agglomération Plaine centrale du Val-de-Marne
2012	*Ernestine building* Immeuble Ernestine	*Restructuring of a building into 27 social housing apartments* Restructuration d'un immeuble en 27 logements sociaux	*Paris (75019), France*	*1,816 m²* 1 816 m²	*Completed* Réalisé	*Paris Habitat*
2012	*Véron-Lepic building* Immeuble Véron-Lepic	*Creation and rehabilitation of 12 apartments at the corner of Rue Véron and Rue Lepic* Création et réhabilitation de 12 logements à l'angle des rues Véron et Lepic *Team: id+ ingénierie (general engineer)* Équipe : id+ ingénierie (ingénierie TCE)	*Paris (75018), France*	*1,000 m²* 1 000 m²	*Completed* Réalisé	*Élogie-SIEMP*
		p. 222				
2012	*Lycee Henri IV student accomodation* Internat du lycée Henri IV	*Creation of boarding facilities for 18 students at the Lycée Henri IV* Création de 18 places d'internat au lycée Henri IV	*Paris (75005), France*	*2,320 m²* 2 320 m²	*Completed* Réalisé	*Île-de-France Region* Région Île-de-France
2012	*Rimbaud Museum* Musée Rimbaud	*Rehabilitation of the Rimbaud Museum* Réhabilitation du musée Rimbaud	*Charleville-Mézières (08), France*	540 m²	*Competition* Concours	*City of Charleville-Mézières* Ville de Charleville-Mézières
2012	*Cultural hub* Pôle culturel	*Construction of a cultural centre, with concert hall, media centre, dance school, fabrication and rehearsal workshops* Construction d'un équipement culturel : salle de spectacles, médiathèque, école de danse, ateliers de fabrication et de répétitions	*Valenciennes (59), France*	*1,262 m²* 1 262 m²	*On hold* Suspendu	*City of Valenciennes* Ville de Valenciennes

2012	*Croix-Rouge neighbourhood contemporary music room* Salle de musiques actuelles du quartier Croix-Rouge	*Construction of a local amenity: music room, community association centre and day nursery for 28 children* Construction d'un équipement de quartier : salle de musique, centre associatif et crèche (28 places)	*Reims (51), France*	*1,795 m²* 1 795 m²	*Competition* Concours	*City of Reims* Ville de Reims
2013	*Reuilly barracks* Caserne de Reuilly	*Transformation, rehabilitation and densification of the Reuilly barracks site, design and urban coordination of 40,000 m² of housing, student housing, a day nursery, artists' studios and retail spaces* Réaménagement, réhabilitation et densification du site de la caserne de Reuilly, conception et coordination urbaine de 40 000 m² construits en logements, résidence étudiante, crèche, ateliers d'artistes, locaux commerciaux	*Paris (75012), France*	*40,000 m²* 40 000 m²	*Completed* Réalisé	*Paris Habitat*
		Team: d&h (landscape), id+ ingénierie (general engineer), BMI (structure engineer), Ingérop (planning, inter-construction management) Équipe : d&h (paysagistes), id+ ingénierie (ingénierie TCE), BMI (ingénierie structure), Ingérop (plannification, gestion interchantiers)				
		p. 280				
2013	*Public spaces of the Reuilly barracks* Espaces publics de la caserne de Reuilly	*Redesign of the public spaces of the Reuilly barracks: garden and squares* Aménagement des espaces publics de la caserne de Reuilly : jardin et places	*Paris (75012), France*	*0.5 ha* 0,5 ha	*Completed* Réalisé	*Paris Habitat*
		Team: d&h (landscape), OGI (exterior infrastructure engineer), ON (lighting) Équipe : d&h (paysagistes), OGI (ingénierie VRD), ON (mise en lumière)				
		p. 288				
2013	*Félix-Faure building* Immeuble Félix-Faure	*Construction of 32 apartments, a retail space and an underground car park. Load-bearing stone construction* Construction de 32 logements, d'un local commercial et d'un parking enterré. Construction en pierre massive semi-porteuse	*Paris (75015), France*	*2,218 m²* 2 218 m²	*Completed* Réalisé	*Cibex*
		Team: Djamo (quantity surveyor, engineer of record), EPDC (structure and mechanical engineer), Diakustic (acoustic engineer) Équipe : Djamo (économiste, maîtrise d'œuvre d'exécution), EPDC (ingénierie structure, fluides), Diakustic (acoustique)				
		p. 210				
2013	*Paul-Meurice building* Immeuble Paul-Meurice	*Construction of a student dormitory of 115 units* Construction d'une résidence étudiante de 115 logements	*Paris (75020), France*	*3,374 m²* 3 374 m²	*Competition* Concours	*RIVP*
2013	*Lycée Joliot-Curie*	*Rehabilitation of the refectory building of the Lycée Joliot-Curie: auditorium, activities and community association rooms* Réhabilitation du réfectoire du lycée Joliot-Curie : auditorium, salles de vie et d'activités associatives	*Dammarie-les-Lys (77), France*	*3,160 m²* 3 160 m²	*Competition* Concours	*Île-de-France Region* Région Île-de-France
2013	*Lorrain Museum* Musée Lorrain	*Renovation, restructuring and extension of the Lorrain Museum* Rénovation, retructuration et extension du musée Lorrain	*Nancy (54), France*	*4,780 m²* 4 780 m²	*Competition* Concours	*City of Nancy* Ville de Nancy
2013	*La Cartoucherie business incubator* Pépinière d'entreprises La Cartoucherie	*Rehabilitation of industrial halls as a business incubator specialising in film animation; creation of digital creation studios, a residential facility, meeting rooms and a data centre* Réhabilitation de halles industrielles en pépinière d'entreprises spécialisées dans les films d'animation ; création de studios de création numérique, d'un foyer, de salles de réunion et d'un *data center*	*Bourg-lès-Valence (26), France*	*2,419 m²* 2 419 m²	*Completed* Réalisé	*Valence-Romans Sud Rhône-Alpes Intermunicipal Community* Communauté d'agglomération Valence-Romans Sud Rhône-Alpes
		Team: id+ ingénierie (general engineer) Équipe : id+ ingénierie (ingénierie TCE)				
		p.162				
2013	*Axima Seitha neighbourhood* Quartier Axima Seitha	*Construction of 338 apartments, student housing and business spaces* Construction de 338 logements, d'une résidence étudiante et de locaux d'activités	*Nantes (44), France*	*30,000 m²* 30 000 m²	*Competition* Concours	*Altarea Cogedim*
2013	*Sainte-Marguerite neighbourhood* Quartier Sainte-Marguerite	*Construction of 140 apartments, a seniors' residence and business spaces* Construction de 140 logements, d'une résidence séniors et de locaux d'activités	*Tours (37), France*	*10,000 m²* 10 000 m²	*Competition* Concours	*Tour(s) Habitat*
2013	*Contemporary music room* Salle de musiques actuelles	*Rehabilitation of a brownfield site as a cultural and music amenity* Réhabilitation d'une friche industrielle en équipement culturel musical	*Charleville-Mézières (08), France*	*2,500 m²* 2 500 m²	*Competition* Concours	*Cœur d'Ardenne Intermunicipal Community* Communauté d'agglomération Cœur d'Ardenne
2014	*Apartment V* Appartement V	*Transformation of an apartment* Réaménagement d'un appartement	*Paris (75012), France*	*77 m²*	*Completed* Réalisé	*Private* Privée

Year	Project	Description	Location	Area	Status	Client
2014	*Denoyez building* Immeuble Denoyez	*Construction of a building with 20 apartments and a day nusery for 50 children* Construction d'un immeuble de 20 logements avec crèche (50 places)	*Paris (75020), France*	*2,250 m²* 2 250 m²	*Competition* Concours	*SIEMP*
2014	*Housing* Logements	*Design of minimal housing models* Conception de modèles de logements minimums	*Shenzhen, China* Shenzhen, Chine	*32 m² each* 32 m² par logement	*Ongoing* En cours	*Vanke*
2014	*Temporary exhibition rooms* Espaces d'expositions temporaires	*Creation of temporary exhibition rooms in the Louvre Museum* Création de salles d'expositions temporaires au musée du Louvre	*Paris (75001), France*	*750 m²*	*Completed* Réalisé	*Louvre Museum* Musée du Louvre
2014	*Maison Saint-Charles*	*Construction of an intergenerational home for a dominican congregation, with 66 apartments and shared spaces; transformation of a chapel into an oratory and training centre* Construction d'un maison intergénérationelle pour une congrégation dominicaine : 66 logements, locaux partagés ; transformation d'une chapelle en oratoire et centre de formation	*Paris (75015), France*	*3,761 m²* 3 761 m²	*Ongoing* En cours	*Vinci Immobilier*
2014	*Yacht club*	*Rehabilitation of a former boathouse as a yacht club* Transformation d'un ancien entrepôt à bateaux en yacht club	*Shenzhen, China* Shenzhen, Chine	*1,200 m²* 1 200 m²	*On hold* Suspendu	*Vanke*
2015	*Arsenal apartment* Appartement Arsenal	*Transformation of an apartment* Réaménagement d'un appartement	*Paris (75004), France*	*70 m²*	*Completed* Réalisé	*Private* Privée
		p. 238				
2015	*Apartment C* Appartement C	*Rehabilitation of an apartment* Réhabilitation d'un appartement	*Sceaux (92), France*	*85 m²*	*Completed* Réalisé	*Private* Privée
2015	*Architecture and Heritage Study Centre* Centre d'interprétation de l'architecture et du patrimoine	*Creation of a cultural centre in the ancient Menier refectory* Création d'un centre culturel dans l'ancien réfectoire Menier	*Noisiel (77), France*	*1,200 m²* 1 200 m²	*Ongoing* En cours	*City of Noisiel* Ville de Noisiel
2015	*Renault design centre* Centre de design industriel Renault	*Transformation of the Renault design centre* Réaménagement des locaux du pôle design de Renault	*Guyancourt (78), France*	*29,000 m²* 29 000 m²	*Competition* Concours	*Renault*
2015	*Castello residential hotel* Résidence hôtelière Castello	*Rehabilitation of the Santa Teresa castle, creation of a residential hotel with 16 apartments, garden, pool, reception, bar and services* Réhabilitation du château de Santa Teresa et création d'une résidence hôtelière : aménagement de 16 appartements, jardin, piscine, réception, bar, services	*Rio de Janeiro, Brazil* Rio de Janeiro, Brésil	*710 m²*	*Completed* Réalisé	*Barlow*
		Team: Marcello Corderio (architect of record), VAC sustentabilidade (mechanical and sustainability engineer) Équipe : Marcello Corderio (architecte local), VAC sustentabilidade (ingénierie fluides et environementale)				
		p. 80				
2015	*Reception of the French National Assembly* Accueil de l'Assemblée nationale	*Renovation and enlargement of the entrance hall of the Palais Bourbon, 128 Rue de l'Université* Rénovation et agrandissement du hall d'entrée du palais Bourbon, 128 rue de l'Université	*Paris (75007), France*	*150 m²*	*Completed* Réalisé	*French National Assembly* Assemblée nationale
		Team: Équilibre Structure (structural engineer), GT2i (mechanical engineer), P. Votruba (quantity surveyor) Équipe : Équilibre Structure (ingénierie structure), GT2i (ingénierie fluides), P. Votruba (économiste)				
		p. 138				
2015	*Métropolis cultural space* Espace culturel Métropolis	*Transformation of the Voltaire electric substation into a cultural space with a cinema, exhibition space, restaurant and video fablab* Transformation de la sous-station électrique Voltaire en espace culturel : cinéma, espace d'exposition, restaurant, fablab vidéo	*Paris (75011), France*	*1,390 m²* 1 390 m²	*Competition* Concours	*Guibor, ARP, Le Pacte*
2015	*Charles B. building* Immeuble Charles B.	*Construction of a building with 23 social housing apartments and 2 retail spaces* Construction d'un immeuble comprenant 23 logements sociaux et 2 commerces	*Fontenay-sous-Bois (94), France*	–	*Ongoing* En cours	*Immobilière 3F*
2015	*Yellow building* Immeuble jaune	*Transformation of an office building into 12 apartments by adding levels* Transformation avec surélévation d'un immeuble de bureaux en 12 logements	*Montreuil (93), France*	*880 m²*	*Completed* Réalisé	*Immobilière 3F*
2015	*Poissonniers building* Immeuble Poissonniers	*Construction of a building with 40 social housing apartments and retail spaces* Construction d'un immeuble comprenant 40 logements sociaux et des locaux commerciaux	*Paris (75018), France*	*2,900 m²* 2 900 m²	*Competition* Concours	*SIEMP*
2015	*La Tour d'Argent building* Immeuble de La Tour d'Argent	*Rehabilitation of the La Tour d'Argent restaurant building* Réhabilitation de l'immeuble du restaurant La Tour d'Argent	*Paris (75005), France*	*2,600 m²* 2 600 m²	*Ongoing* En cours	*La Tour d'Argent*

2015	*Building for the ZAC du Mail local government project* Immeuble de la ZAC du Mail	*Construction of a 34-apartments building with studios* Construction d'un immeuble de 34 logements avec ateliers	*Rennes (35), France*	*2,830 m²* 2 830 m²	*Competition* Concours	*Lamotte*
2015	*Maison Renault*	*Restructuring of a building with a reception area, auditorium and exhibition space* Restructuration d'un bâtiment en espace de réception, auditorium et espace d'exposition	*Boulogne-Billancourt (92), France*	*1,540 m²* 1 540 m²	*Competition* Concours	*Renault*
2015	*Cast Iron House playroom* Salle de jeu Cast Iron House	*Creation of a children's playroom* Aménagement d'une salle de jeu pour enfants	*New York, United States* New York, États-Unis	*62 m²*	*Competition* Concours	*Knightsbridge Properties Corp*
2015	*Éole Évangile neighbourhood* Quartier Éole Évangile	*Construction of a 40,000 m² ensemble composed of housing, hotels, logistical spaces, a café, a fablab, retail spaces and a sports centre* Construction d'un ensemble immobilier : logements, hôtels, espace logistique, café, fablab, commerces, centre sportif	*Paris (75020), France*	*40,000 m²* 40 000 m²	*Competition* Concours	*Marignan Spie Batignolles*
2015	*Gastronomic Villa Medicis* Villa Médicis de la gastronomie	*Creation of a gastronomic training and research centre, with a restaurant, at the Hôtel de Coulanges* Création d'un centre de gastronomie, de formation et de recherche avec restaurant à l'hôtel de Coulanges	*Paris (75004), France*	*2,633 m²* 2 633 m²	*Competition* Concours	*Sogeprom*
2016	*Urban development* Aménagement urbain	*Spatial development, urban furniture, signage and creative lighting for the town centre* Aménagement urbain, mobilier urbain, signalétique et mise en lumière du centre-ville	*Mehun-sur-Yèvre (18), France*	*3.2 ha* 3,2 ha	*Completed* Réalisé	*City of Mehun-sur-Yèvre* Ville de Mehun-sur-Yèvre
2016	*Abbey church surroundings* Abords de l'abbatiale	*Improvements to the forecourt and surroundings of the abbey church* Aménagement du parvis et des abords de l'abbatiale	*Saint-Pierre-sur-Dives (14), France*	*0.3 ha* 0,3 ha	*Completed* Réalisé	*City of Saint-Pierre-sur-Dives* Ville de Saint-Pierre-sur-Dives
2016	*Main courtyard of the French National Assembly* Cour d'honneur de l'Assemblée nationale	*Redesign of the main courtyard of the Palais Bourbon and design of specific furniture* Aménagement de la cour d'honneur du palais Bourbon, conception de mobiliers spécifiques *Team: OGI and BET Parker (engineers)* Équipe : OGI et BET Parker (ingénierie)	*Paris (75007), France*	*4,150 m²* 4 150 m²	*Completed* Réalisé	*French National Assembly* Assemblée nationale
		p. 40, 128				
2016	*Bessières building* Immeuble Bessières	*Construction of 16 apartments and a business space* Construction de 16 logements et d'un local d'activités	*Paris (75017), France*	*715 m²*	*Competition* Concours	*Pierres et Lumières*
2016	*Black building* Immeuble noir	*Construction of approx. 20 apartments* Construction d'environ 20 logements	*Montreuil (93), France*	*1,076 m²* 1 076 m²	*Ongoing* En cours	*OPH Montreuil*
2016	*Red building* Immeuble rouge	*Construction of approx. 15 apartments* Construction d'environ 15 logements	*Montreuil (93), France*	*935 m²*	*Ongoing* En cours	*OPH Montreuil*
2016	*Housing buildings, Square Quentin* Immeubles square Quentin	*Construction of 31 rental apartments and rehabilitation of 86 occupied apartments* Construction de 31 logements collectifs locatifs et réhabilitation de 86 logements occupés	*Rennes (35), France*	*6,479 m²* 6 479 m²	*Ongoing* En cours	*Archipel Habitat*
2016	*National Audiovisual Institute* Institut national de l'audiovisuel	*Partial reconfiguration of the BRY 1 building at the National Audiovisual Institute* Réaménagement partiel du bâtiment BRY 1 de l'Institut national de l'audiovisuel *Team: id+ ingénierie (general engineer), Impédance (acoustic engineer), ON (lighting)* Équipe : id+ ingénierie (ingénierie TCE), Impédance (acoustique), ON (mise en lumière)	*Bry-sur-Marne (94), France*	*5,900 m²* 5 900 m²	*Completed* Réalisé	*National Audiovisual Institute, OPPIC representative* Institut national de l'audiovisuel (INA), OPPIC mandataire
		p. 178				
2016	*Micro-Folie* Micro-folie	*Construction of an ephemeral cultural establishment composed of 3 modules: digital exhibition room/performance space, reception area/cooperative bar, fablab; reproducible and adaptable for other sites* Construction d'un établissement culturel éphémère constitué de 3 modules : une salle d'exposition numérique/espace scénique, un accueil/bar coopératif, un fablab ; principe reproductible et adaptable à d'autre sites *Team: Bernard Tschumi (architect), VPEAS (quantity surveyor)* Équipe : Bernard Tschumi (architecte), VPEAS (économiste)	*Sevran (93), France*	*250 m²*	*Completed* Réalisé	*La Villette Public Gardens and Exhibition Hall* Établissement public du parc et de la grande halle de la Villette (EPPGHV)
		p. 116				

2016	*Paris Museum of Modern Art* Musée d'Art moderne de Paris	*Partial renovation of the museum* Rénovation partielle du musée	*Paris (75016), France*	*21,000 m^2* 21 000 m^2	*Completed* Réalisé	*City of Paris, DPA (Heritage and Architecture Department)* Ville de Paris, DPA (Direction du patrimoine et de l'architecture)
		Team: Équilibre Structure (structural engineer), VPEAS (quantity surveyor), GT2i (mechanical engineer), Studio GGSV (furniture design), Métronome (site organisation and monitoring), Atelier On (lighting), Labeyrie (multimedia), Terrasol (geo-technician), Aubry & Guiguet (programme), Risk & Co (public and museum safety), Thierry Cames (fire safety coordination) Équipe: Équilibre Structure (ingénierie structure), VPEAS (économiste), GT2i (bureau d'études fluides), Studio GGSV (design mobilier), Métronome (organisation et pilotage chantier), Atelier On (éclairagiste), Labeyrie (multimédia), Terrasol (géotechnicien), Aubry & Guiguet (programmiste), Risk & Co (sûreté et sécurité des publics), Thierry Cames (coordonnateur SSI)				
		p. 100				
2016	*Social hub* Pôle social	*Rehabilitation of an industrial site for the creation of a social hub* Réhabilitation d'un site industriel pour créer un pôle social	*Beaugency (45), France*	*2,105 m^2* 2 105 m^2	*Competition* Concours	*City of Beaugency* Ville de Beaugency
2016	*Davout neighbourhood* Quartier Davout	*Redevelopment and rehabilitation of the Davout-Félix-Terrier housing estate and its surroundings (728 apartments, 39 staircases)* Requalification et réhabilitation de l'ensemble immobilier Davout-Félix-Terrier et de ses abords (728 logements, 39 escaliers)	*Paris (75020), France*	*5,698 m^2* 5 698 m^2	*Ongoing* En cours	*Paris Habitat*
2017	*Sciences Po campus* Campus de Sciences Po	*Restructuring of the Hôtel de l'Artillerie site for Sciences Po's urban campus* Restructuration du site de l'hôtel de l'Artillerie en campus urbain pour Sciences Po	*Paris (75007), France*	*14,200 m^2* 14 200 m^2	*Competition* Concours	*Icade*
2017	*Sports complex* Complexe sportif	*Construction of a sports complex: stadium, running track, multi-sports rooms, gymnasium, bowling alley* Construction d'un complexe sportif : stade, piste d'athlétisme, salles multisport, gymnase, bowling	*Clamart (92), France*	*22,553 m^2* 22 553 m^2	*Competition* Concours	*City of Clamart* Ville de Clamart
2017	*Two buildings* Deux immeubles	*Construction of 50 apartments: a 25-apartment home for mentally handicapped people, 25 social housing apartments, and shared spaces* Construction de 50 logements : 25 logements pour un foyer de personnes handicapées mentales et 25 logements sociaux ; espaces partagés	*Chambray-lès-Tours (37), France*	*2,700 m^2* 2 700 m^2	*Competition* Concours	*Touraine Logements*
2017	*Pelterie building* Immeuble Pelterie	*Construction of 30 social housing apartments, a craft workshop, and a car park* Construction de 30 logements sociaux, d'un local artisanal et d'un parking	*Boulogne-Billancourt (92), France*	*2,512 m^2* 2 512 m^2	*Competition* Concours	*Hauts-de-Seine Habitat*
2017	*Énergie building* Immeuble Énergie	*Rehabilitation of the Énergie building for the creation of a business incubator* Réhabilitation de l'immeuble Énergie en pépinière d'entreprises	*Amnéville (57), France*	*1,900 m^2* 1 900 m^2	*Competition* Concours	*Joint Association Leading Studies and Developments of the Portes de l'Orne, EPF Lorraine* Syndicat mixte d'études et d'aménagement des Portes de l'Orne, Établissement public foncier de Lorraine
2017	*Trudaine building and day nursery* Immeuble et crèche Trudaine	*Creation of offices, housing and a day nursery* Création de bureaux, de logements et d'une crèche	*Paris (75009), France*	*8,823 m^2* 8 823 m^2	*Competition* Concours	*Finapar, Naccarat*
2017	*Jean-Macé building* Immeuble Jean-Macé	*Transformation of the Lycée Jean-Macé into a 73-room hotel and 167 apartments* Transformation du lycée Jean-Macé en 167 logements et un hôtel de 73 chambres	*Lille (59), France*	*14,833 m^2* 14 833 m^2	*Competition* Concours	*Finapar, Melt*
2017	*Malevart building* Immeuble Malevart	*Transformation of a car park into an innovative office building and urban logistics centre in Villa du Clos de Malevart* Transformation d'un garage en immeuble de bureaux innovant et centre de logistique urbaine, Villa du Clos de Malevart	*Paris (75011), France*	*3,280 m^2* 3 280 m^2	*Ongoing* En cours	*Galia*
		Team: EVP (structural engineer), B52 (mechanical engineer), Impédance (acoustic engineer), Casso (fire safety consultant), VPEAS (quantity surveyor), Karolina Samborska (landscape) Équipe : EVP (ingénierie structure), B52 (ingénierie génie climatique, fluides), Impédance (acoustique), Casso (prévention incendie), VPEAS (économiste), Karolina Samborska (paysagiste)				
		p. 308				
2017	*Philippe-de-Girard building* Immeuble Philippe-de-Girard	*Creation of 10 apartments and an upcycling centre* Création de 10 logements et d'une ressourcerie	*Paris (75010), France*	*1,315 m^2* 1 315 m^2	*Competition* Concours	*RIVP*

Year	Project	Description	Location	Area	Status	Client
2017	*Pleyel building* Immeuble Pleyel	*Construction of a hybrid office building including a cultural incubator; rehabilitation of an urban factory for the creation of a culinary incubator, a café-concert, laboratories and dance studios* Construction d'un immeuble de bureaux hybride intégrant un incubateur culturel ; réhabilitation d'une usine urbaine en incubateur culinaire, café-concert, laboratoires et studios de danse	*Saint-Denis (93), France*	*7,300 m²* 7 300 m²	*Competition* Concours	*Covivio*
		Team: OMA (urban planning), Transsolar (climate engineer), Rotor (reuse consultant), Setec tpi (structure engineer), Barbanel (mechanical engineer), Agi2d (sustainability engineer), DAL (quantity surveyor), Le Sens de la Ville (programme) Équipe : OMA (urbaniste), Transsolar (ingénierie climat), Rotor (ingénierie réemploi), Setec tpi (ingénierie structure), Barbanel (ingénierie fluides), Agi2d (ingénierie développement durable), DAL (économiste), Le Sens de la Ville (programmiste)				
		p. 58				
2017	*Housing and hotel* Logements et hôtel	*Construction of 63 apartments, a day nursery, and a luxury hotel with 44 rooms giving onto the castle grounds* Construction de 63 logements, d'une crèche et d'un hôtel de luxe de 44 chambres en front du parc du château	*Versailles (78), France*	*13,350 m²* 13 350 m²	*Competition* Concours	*Kaufman & Broad*
2017	*Vauban buildings* Immeubles Vauban	*Construction of 162 apartments, a day nursery, professional offices and a car park* Construction de 162 logements, d'une crèche, de locaux professionnels et d'un parking	*Versailles (78), France*	*9,380 m²* 9 380 m²	*Competition* Concours	*City of Versailles, Finapar, Hyatt* Ville de Versailles, Finapar, Hyatt
2017	*Guest house* Maison des hôtes	*Construction of a guest house in an abbey* Construction d'une maison des hôtes dans une abbaye	*Bec-Hellouin (27), France*	*1,534 m²* 1 534 m²	*Ongoing* En cours	*Friends of the Bec Association* Association des amis du Bec
2017	*National Maritime Museum* Musée national de la Marine	*Renovation of the museum inside the Palais de Chaillot* Rénovation du musée au sein du palais de Chaillot	*Paris (75016), France*	*10,500 m²* 10 500 m²	*Ongoing* En cours	*Musée de la Marine, OPPIC representative* Musée de la Marine, OPPIC mandataire
		Team: Snohetta (associate architect), Équilibre Structure (structural engineer), Igrec Ingénierie (mechanical and sustainability engineer) Équipe : Snohetta (architecte associé), Équilibre Structure (ingénierie structure), Igrec Ingénierie (ingénierie génie climatique, fluides, développement durable et exploitation-maintenance)				
		p. 296				
2017	*Palais de Tokyo forecourt* Parvis du Palais de Tokyo	*Partial renovation of the forecourt* Rénovation partielle du parvis	*Paris (75016), France*	*1 ha*	*Completed* Réalisé	*OPPIC*
2017	*Castle pavilion* Pavillon du château	*Construction of a pavilion serving as a reception space, ticket office and boutique for the castle* Construction d'un pavillon d'accueil, billetterie et boutique pour le château	*Dinan (22), France*	*115 m²*	*Completed* Réalisé	*City of Dinan* Ville de Dinan
2017	*Business incubator* Pépinière d'entreprises	*Construction of a business incubator, art and craft workshop, exhibition space, fablab* Construction d'une pépinière d'entreprises, avec atelier de création, espace de présentation, fablab	*Pantin (93), France*	*5,177 m²* 5 177 m²	*Competition* Concours	*RIVP*
2017	*Place de la Madeleine*	*Redesign of the square with design of urban furniture* Aménagement de la place avec conception d'un mobilier urbain	*Paris (75008), France*	*2.8 ha* 2,8 ha	*Completed* Réalisé	*City of Paris, DVD (Roads and Transport Department)* Ville de Paris, DVD (Direction de la voirie et des déplacements)
		Team: OGI (exterior infrastructure engineer, quantity surveyor), Emma Blanc (landscape), Muriel Pagès (bike consultant), Iris Conseil (mobility and traffic lights) Équipe : OGI (ingénierie VRD, économiste), Emma Blanc (paysagiste), Muriel Pagès (expert plan vélo), Iris Conseil (ingénierie mobilité, SLT)				
		p. 88				
2017	*Cultural hub* Pôle culturel	*Creation of a cultural hub in the former archbishop's palace, media centre, music school, Centre for Architectural and Heritage Studies* Création d'un pôle culturel dans l'ancien archevêché : médiathèque, école de musique, Centre d'interprétation de l'architecture et du patrimoine	*Embrun (05), France*	*1,900 m²* 1 900 m²	*Ongoing* En cours	*City of Embrun* Ville d'Embrun
2017	*Bois Perrin neighbourhood* Quartier Bois Perrin	*Transformation and densification of the old hospital site: 450 apartments, 400-unit underground car park, a day nursery, a park and business spaces* Transformation et densification du site de l'ancien hôpital : 450 logements, parking enterré de 400 places, crèche, parc, locaux d'activités	*Rennes (35), France*	*3.7 ha* 3,7 ha	*Ongoing* En cours	*City of Rennes* Ville de Rennes
2017	*Renault branch* Succursale de Renault	*Rehabilitation and redesign of a branch of Renault* Réhabilitation et concept d'aménagement d'une succursale de Renault	*Buc (78), France*	*5,550 m²* 5 550 m²	*Competition* Concours	*Renault*
2017	*Studio Louvre*	*Creation of an artistic and cultural centre at the Louvre, with a forum and teaching and training workshops* Création d'un centre artistique et culturel avec forum, ateliers de formation et ateliers pédagogiques au musée du Louvre	*Paris (75001), France*	*1,265 m²* 1 265 m²	*Ongoing* En cours	*Louvre museum* Musée du Louvre

2018	*Surroundings of Notre-Dame-en-Vaux* Abords de la cathédrale Notre-Dame-en-Vaux	*Redevelopment of the Notre-Dame block in the town centre* Aménagement urbain du centre-ville, îlot Notre-Dame	*Châlons-en-Champagne (51), France*	*2.8 ha* 2,8 ha	*Competition* Concours	*City of Châlons-en-Champagne* Ville de Châlons-en-Champagne
2018	*Apartment B* Appartement B	*Addition of a level to an existing building* Surélévation d'un immeuble	*Paris (75008), France*	*217 m²*	*Ongoing* En cours	*Private* Privée
2018	*Kellerman military barracks* Caserne Kellerman	*Rehabilitation of the Kellerman barracks and improvements to public space* Réhabilitation de la caserne Kellerman, aménagement des espaces publics	*Châteaudun (28), France*	*6,541 m²* 6 541 m²	*Competition* Concours	*City of Châteaudun, Châteaudun Social Housing Office, Châteaudun Hospital* Ville de Châteaudun, OPH du Grand Châteaudun, Hôpital de Châteaudun
2018	*City of Creative Economics and Digital Engineering* Cité de l'économie créative et de l'ingénierie numérique	*Construction of a digital city* Construction d'une cité numérique	*Chalon-sur-Saône (71), France*	*1,958 m²* 1 958 m²	*Competition* Concours	*Greater Chalon* Le Grand Chalon
2018	*Ars campus office building* Immeuble de bureaux du campus de l'Ars	*Construction of a campus composed of offices, workshops, start-up spaces, coworking spaces and a café* Construction d'un campus de bureaux, avec atelier, espace start-up, espaces de coworking et café	*Bordeaux (33), France*	*18,980 m²* 18 980 m²	*Competition* Concours	*Covivio, OnePoint*
2018	*M9A building* Immeuble M9A	*Construction of the University of Chicago's, Second Home premises, and 80 apartments* Construction de l'université de Chicago, des locaux de Second Home et de 80 logements	*Paris (75013), France*	*9,317 m²* 9 317 m²	*Competition* Concours	*Crédit Agricole Immobilier, Engie*
2018	*Îlot Saint-Germain buildings* Immeubles îlot Saint-Germain	*Rehabilitation and restructuring of office buildings into 280 social housing apartments inside the former French Army Ministry building* Réhabilitation et restructuration d'immeubles de bureaux en 280 logements sociaux au sein de l'ancien ministère des Armées	*Paris (75007), France*	*11,552 m²* 11 552 m²	*Ongoing* En cours	*RIVP*
2018	*House of Cosmetics* Maison de la cosmétique	*Creation of the International House of Cosmetics, opposite the cathedral* Création de la Maison internationale de la cosmétique, face à la cathédrale	*Chartres (28), France*	*2,068 m²* 2 068 m²	*Competition* Concours	*Chartres Métropole Intermunicipal Community* Communauté d'agglomération Chartres Métropole
2018	*Bossage furniture* Mobilier Bossage	*Urban furniture designed as a defense against ramming by cars, as part of Faire Design Paris 2018* Conception de mobilier urbain de défense contre les voitures-béliers, dans le cadre de Faire Design Paris 2018	*Paris (75), France*	–	*Ongoing* En cours	*City of Paris* Ville de Paris
2018	*CMA CGM Museum* Musée CMA CGM	*Construction of the CMA CGM Museum* Construction du musée CMA CGM	*Marseille (13), France*	*380 m²*	*Ongoing* En cours	*CMA CGM*
2018	*Capuchin Museum* Musée des Capucins	*Extension and rehabilitation of the city museum and the House of Brie Cheese in the Capuchin monastery* Extension et réhabilitation du musée municipal et création de la Maison des fromages de Brie au sein du couvent des Capucins	*Coulommiers (77), France*	*2,360 m²* 2 360 m²	*Competition* Concours	*City of Coulommiers, Coulommiers Pays de Brie Intermunicipal Community* Ville de Coulommiers, Communauté d'agglomération Coulommiers Pays de Brie
2018	*MAM's restaurant* Restaurant MAM's	*Interior design of the restaurant inside the Paris Museum of Modern Art (MAM)* Aménagement intérieur du restaurant du musée d'Art moderne (MAM) de Paris	*Paris (75016), France*	*680 m²*	*On hold* Suspendu	*Moma Group*
2019	*Right wing of the Familistère* Aile droite du familistère	*Transformation of the right wing into 65 social housing apartments and shared spaces* Transformation de l'aile droite en 65 logements sociaux et en espaces partagés	*Guise (02), France*	*8,300 m²* 8 300 m²	*Ongoing* En cours	*CDC Logements*
2019	*Louvre Carrousel* Carrousel du Louvre	*Redesign of shared spaces for the maintenance of the collections in the Louvre Museum* Aménagement d'espaces mutualisés de traitement des collections du musée du Louvre	*Paris (75001), France*	*1,900 m²* 1 900 m²	*Ongoing* En cours	*Louvre Museum* Musée du Louvre
2019	*La Cabotte wine storehouse* Cuverie de La Cabotte	*Extension of the estate's vat house* Extension de la cuverie du domaine viticole	*Mondragon (26), France*	*250 m²*	*Ongoing* En cours	*La Cabotte*
2019	*Coty buildings* Immeubles Coty	*Construction of 35 apartments and 6 individual houses, an underground car park and a medical centre* Construction de 35 logements et 6 maisons individuelles, d'un parking enterré et d'un centre médical	*Tours (37), France*	*3,300 m²* 3 300 m²	*Ongoing* En cours	*Covivio*
2019	*Lota house* Maison Lota	*Construction of an individual house next to a private mansion* Construction d'une maison individuelle accolée à un hôtel particulier	*Paris (75016), France*	*153 m²*	*Ongoing* En cours	*Private* Privée
2019	*Quille furniture* Mobilier Quille	*Design of a furniture base for multiple uses* Conception d'un piétement en bois assemblable pour usages multiples	–	–	*Completed* Réalisé	*In-house production* Autoproduction
		p. 50				

2019	*Table tubes furniture* Mobilier Table tubes	*Design of a modular table base with luminous extensions* Conception d'un piétement de table modulaire avec extensions lumineuses	–	–	*Ongoing* En cours	*Compagnie*
2019	*Rolin Museum* Musée Rolin	*Renovation and extension of the Rolin Museum* Rénovation et extension du musée Rolin	*Autun (71), France*	*4,649 m²* 4 649 m²	*Competition* Concours	*City of Autun* Ville d'Autun
2019	*Nef on Île des Vannes* Nef des Vannes	*Transformation of the Grande Nef on the Île des Vannes into a performance space and sports training centre* Transformation de la grande nef de l'île des Vannes en espace de spectacles et centre d'entraînement sportif	*Saint-Ouen (93), France*	*20,620 m²* 20 620 m²	*Competition* Concours	*Solideo*
2019	*MUE itinerant pavilion* Pavillon itinérant MUE	*Creation of an educational pavilion for the university* Création d'un pavillon universitaire de l'éducation	*Besançon (25), France*	*30 m²*	*Ongoing* En cours	*Besançon Education Authority* Rectorat de Besançon
		p. 316				
2019	*Well of Science* Puits de Sciences	*Construction of the Well of Science, with exhibition spaces, interpretation centre, coworking spaces* Construction d'un centre culturel avec espaces d'exposition, centre d'interprétation, espaces de coworking	*Gardanne (13), France*	*5,435 m²* 5 435 m²	*Ongoing* En cours	*Public Development Organisation for Gardanne and its Region* Société d'économie mixte d'aménagement de Gardanne et de sa région
2019	*Cash neighbourhood* Quartier Cash	*Partial transformation of the Cash hospital and creation of 117 apartments, a medical centre and a car park* Transformation partielle de l'hôpital Cash et création de 117 logements, d'un centre médical et d'un parking	*Nanterre (92), France*	*9,290 m²* 9 290 m²	*Competition* Concours	*Altarea Cogedim*
2019	*Chapelle-Charbon neighbourhood* Quartier Chapelle-Charbon	*Design of the Chapelle-Charbon urban project: 430 apartments, commercial spaces, a school and public spaces* Conception du projet urbain du quartier Chapelle-Charbon : 430 logements, locaux d'activités, école et espaces publics	*Paris (75018), France*	*35,000 m²* 35 000 m²	*Ongoing* En cours	*Paris Métropole & Aménagement*
2019	*Tolbiac-Moulinet neighbourhood* Quartier Tolbiac-Moulinet	*Construction of 167 apartments, a day nursery, fair trade businesses; rehabilitation of 44 homes; planning coordination of the site as a whole* Construction de 167 logements, d'une crèche, de commerces solidaires et réhabilitation de 44 logements ; coordination urbaine de l'ensemble	*Paris (75013), France*	*14,340 m²* 14 340 m²	*Pending* En attente	*Paris Habitat*
2020	*Alpha training centre* Centre de formation Alpha	*Transformation of the entrance hall of the National Audiovisual Institute for the Alpha training centre* Réaménagement du hall d'accueil de l'Institut national de l'audiovisuel pour le centre de formation Alpha	*Bry-sur-Marne (94), France*	*550 m²*	*Ongoing* En cours	*National Audiovisual Institute* Institut national de l'audiovisuel (INA)
2020	*Wilson building* Immeuble Wilson	*Construction of 30 apartements and the Toy Museum* Construction de 30 logements et du musée du Jouet	*Le Pré-Saint-Gervais (93), France*	*2,200 m²* 2 200 m²	*Ongoing* En cours	*Altarea Cogedim*
2020	*Château de la Maye building* Immeuble du château de la Maye	*Construction of 60 apartments with car park on the Château de la Maye site* Construction de 60 logements avec parking au château de la Maye	*Versailles (78), France*	*5,700 m²* 5 700 m²	*Pending* En attente	*Linkcity*
2020	*Clichy building* Immeuble Clichy	*Construction of 48 apartments, shared spaces and a car park* Construction de 48 logements, d'espaces partagés et d'un parking	*Clichy-sous-Bois (93), France*	*2,100 m²* 2 100 m²	*Competition* Concours	*Batigère*
2020	*Individual house* Maison individuelle	*Construction of an individual house* Construction d'une maison individuelle	*Les Petites-Dalles (76), France*	*140 m²*	*Ongoing* En cours	*Private* Privée
2020	*Slavery Museum* Musée de l'Esclavage	*Construction of the Plantation Society and Slavery Museum* Construction du musée de la Société de plantation et de l'Esclavage	*Villèle (97), Reunion Island* Villèle (97), La Réunion	*2,900 m²* 2 900 m²	*Ongoing* En cours	*Reunion Island Department* Département de La Réunion
2020	*Vernon Museum* Musée de Vernon	*Restructuring of the museum, including a space for impressionists* Restructuration du musée intégrant un espace des impressionnistes	*Vernon (23), France*	*1,150 m²* 1 150 m²	*Competition* Concours	*Normandie Axe Seine*
2020	*Sciences Po learning centre* Learning center de Sciences Po	*Rehabilitation of a building as a learning centre for Sciences Po* Réhabilitation d'un bâtiment en *learning center* pour Sciences Po	*Saint-Germain-en-Laye (78), France*	*1,942 m²* 1 942 m²	*Ongoing* En cours	*Yvelines Department* Département des Yvelines

Annexes

h2o architectes is dedicated to architectural, heritage and urban creation and reprogramming. Structured as a collective whose rich resources lie in its different identities, the office develops programmes ranging in type and scale from housing to cultural amenities to public space. Unsurprisingly, the historical and social complexity of contexts such as these has given rise to a real suppleness of approach.

The projects are purposefully open-ended, the aim being nuanced, ongoing interaction with a pre-existing setting that is at once re-examined, disrupted and enriched. Moreover, the programme itself is challenged as a means of looking beyond the initial requirements to the emergence of regenerated living spaces offering a fresh historical perspective. The formal outcome is overtly committed, providing for appropriation without necessarily specifying its character.

The office's work has been the subject of colloquia, exhibitions and publications in France and abroad, and has won awards including the Nouveaux Albums des Jeunes Architectes et des Paysagistes and Europe 40 under 40.

h2o architectes est une agence de création et de reprogrammation architecturale, patrimoniale et urbaine. Elle développe des programmes variés à différentes échelles, allant du logement à l'espace public en passant par les équipements culturels. L'agence s'est construite comme un collectif aux différentes identités qui font sa richesse. La complexité des contextes abordés tant historiquement que socialement a naturellement développé une agilité dans sa démarche.

Les projets sont conçus de manière ouverte. Il s'agit de les inscrire dans un dialogue fin avec leur environnement, dans la continuité d'une situation préexistante qui est réinterrogée, perturbée, enrichie... Le programme est lui aussi questionné pour dépasser la demande et faire émerger des lieux renouvelés. Ces espaces à vivre proposent une nouvelle histoire. La forme créée est volontairement engagée, prévoyant l'appropriation sans en déterminer nécessairement la nature spécifique.

Les travaux de l'agence ont fait l'objet de conférences, expositions et publications en France et à l'étranger. Parmi divers prix et récompenses, h2o architectes a été lauréat des Nouveaux Albums des jeunes architectes et des paysagistes et lauréat du prix Europe 40 under 40.

Associated architects

Charlotte Hubert

Graduated from the Paris-Belleville National School of Architecture in 1999, École de Chaillot in 2003. Chief Architect Historic Monuments Department since 2016. Member of the Commission Nationale du Patrimoine et de l'Architecture since 2007. Lecturer at the École Nationale Supérieure d'Architecture in Nancy, 2011–2016. Currently lecturing at the University of Angers. Created h2o architectes with Jean-Jacques Hubert, 2005. Laureate Nouveaux Albums des Jeunes Architectes et des Paysagistes, 2008. In 2016, with Jean-Jacques Hubert and Antoine Santiard, created Eugène Architectes du Patrimoine, specialising in the restoration of historic monuments.

Jean-Jacques Hubert

Graduated from the Nantes National School of Architecture in 1999. Teacher at the École Supérieure des Arts et Techniques, Paris, 2006–2010. Associate author at "Dess(e)ins", creative drawing observatory, since 2012. Created h2o architectes with Charlotte Hubert, 2005. Laureate Nouveaux Albums des Jeunes Architectes et des Paysagistes, 2008. In 2016, with Charlotte Hubert and Antoine Santiard, created Eugène Architectes du Patrimoine, specialising in the restoration of historic monuments.

Antoine Santiard

Architect, graduated from the École Polytechnique Fédérale in Lausanne in 2001. Teacher at the Paris-Val de Seine National School of Architecture, 2010–2012 and Paris-Malaquais, 2007–2010. Has been teaching on the New York/Paris programme at the Graduate School of Architecture, Planning and Preservation, Columbia University since 2012. Joined h2o architectes as a partner, 2008. In 2016, with Charlotte Hubert and Jean-Jacques Hubert, created Eugène Architectes du Patrimoine, specialising in the restoration of historic monuments.

Architectes associés

Charlotte Hubert

Architecte DPLG, diplômée de l'École nationale supérieure d'architecture de Paris-Belleville en 1999, diplômée de l'École de Chaillot en 2003, architecte en chef des Monuments historiques depuis 2016. Membre de la Commission nationale du patrimoine et de l'architecture depuis 2007. Enseignante associée à l'université d'Angers, après être intervenue au sein de l'École nationale supérieure d'architecture de Nancy de 2011 à 2016. A créé h2o architectes avec Jean-Jacques Hubert en 2005. Lauréate des Nouveaux Albums des jeunes architectes et des paysagistes 2008. A créé en 2016 Eugène architectes du patrimoine, structure spécialisée dans la restauration des monuments historiques, avec Jean-Jacques Hubert et Antoine Santiard.

Jean-Jacques Hubert

Architecte DPLG, diplômé de l'École nationale d'architecture de Nantes en 1999. Enseignant à l'École supérieure des arts et techniques, studio d'architecture à Paris de 2006 à 2010. Auteur associé au projet « Dess(e)ins », observatoire des dessins liés aux processus créatifs, depuis 2012. A créé h2o architectes avec Charlotte Hubert en 2005. Lauréat des Nouveaux Albums des jeunes architectes et des paysagistes 2008. A créé en 2016 Eugène architectes du patrimoine, structure spécialisée dans la restauration des monuments historiques, avec Charlotte Hubert et Antoine Santiard.

Antoine Santiard

Architecte EPFL, diplômé de l'École polytechnique fédérale de Lausanne en 2001. Enseignant à l'ENSA de Paris-Val de Seine de 2010 à 2012 et à celle de Paris-Malaquais de 2007 à 2010. Enseignant dans le cadre du programme New York/Paris à la Graduate School of Architecture, Planning and Preservation, Columbia University depuis 2012. A rejoint h2o architectes en tant qu'associé en 2008. A créé en 2016 Eugène architectes du patrimoine, structure spécialisée dans la restauration des monuments historiques, avec Charlotte et Jean-Jacques Hubert.

Partners
Noémie Bercot, administrator
Nestor Ivanov, architect

Architects
Joëlle Agarande, Paul Boileau,
Adélaïde Breuvart, Clément Dauvilliers,
Charles Derilleux-Bes, Thomas Ducher,
Anouk Foch, Damien Fregefond,
Lise Hémard, Céline Lebreton,
Marie d'Oncieu, Mathilde Reiss,
Lucie Rossignol

Collaborations since 2008
Ghita Aaddaj (architect), Jonathan Alotto (architect), Sam Aly Goda (architect), Joachim Badaoui, Pauline Besançon, Yann Beuzit, Charlyne Bourin, Beatriz Campos, Arnaud Cesar, Tiffany Chu, Clara Corominas Gener, Mathieu Crabouillet, Océane Dehaynain, Tristan Delagneau, Rudy Dieudonne, Alice Dufourmantelle (architect), Claire Fachetti, Marcello Ferrara (architect), Fanette Fressynet, Pierre Gaboriaud, François Gastesoleil, Pierre Gommier (architect), Aurélien Gosset (architect), Nicolas Grillet, Baptiste Guastavino, Alexandra Guiot (administration), Montserrat Guzman (architect), Laure Hamelin (architect), Bumjin Kim, Jieun Kim, Ange Lemée, Erwan Le Meur, Marie Lennon (architect), Cyrielle Leonard, Malgorzata Los (architect), Martial Marquet (architect), Léo Martial, Nicolas Maugery, Mathieu Moncomble, Julien Paulus (architect), Ilaria Peru, Vanille Pfeffer, Laurent Pottier (architect), Krzysztof Pydo, Lucie Réau (architect), Camille Renault (architect), Godefroy Saint-Georges, Loredana Salavastru, Clara Salinas Álvarez, Léo Sandoz, Esther Sélo (architect), Katharina Westphalen

Partenaires
Noémie Bercot, responsable administrative
Nestor Ivanov, architecte

Architectes
Joëlle Agarande, Paul Boileau,
Adélaïde Breuvart, Clément Dauvilliers,
Charles Derilleux-Bes, Thomas Ducher,
Anouk Foch, Damien Fregefond,
Lise Hémard, Céline Lebreton,
Marie d'Oncieu, Mathilde Reiss,
Lucie Rossignol

Collaborations depuis 2008
Ghita Aaddaj (architecte), Jonathan Alotto (architecte), Sam Aly Goda (architecte), Joachim Badaoui, Pauline Besançon, Yann Beuzit, Charlyne Bourin, Beatriz Campos, Arnaud Cesar, Tiffany Chu, Clara Corominas Gener, Mathieu Crabouillet, Océane Dehaynain, Tristan Delagneau, Rudy Dieudonne, Alice Dufourmantelle (architecte), Claire Fachetti, Marcello Ferrara (architecte), Fanette Fressynet, Pierre Gaboriaud, François Gastesoleil, Pierre Gommier (architecte), Aurélien Gosset (architecte), Nicolas Grillet, Baptiste Guastavino, Alexandra Guiot (administration), Montserrat Guzman (architecte), Laure Hamelin (architecte), Bumjin Kim, Jieun Kim, Ange Lemée, Erwan Le Meur, Marie Lennon (architecte), Cyrielle Leonard, Malgorzata Los (architecte), Martial Marquet (architecte), Léo Martial, Nicolas Maugery, Mathieu Moncomble, Julien Paulus (architecte), Ilaria Peru, Vanille Pfeffer, Laurent Pottier (architecte), Krzysztof Pydo, Lucie Réau (architecte), Camille Renault (architecte), Godefroy Saint-Georges, Loredana Salavastru, Clara Salinas Álvarez, Léo Sandoz, Esther Sélo (architecte), Katharina Westphalen

Thanks

Charlotte Hubert, Jean-Jacques Hubert and Antoine Santiard would like to thank all the h2o architectes collaborators for their unfailing energy. They would also like to thank for their faith: Bruno Airaud, Artefactory, the French National Assembly, Julien Attard, Jean-Pierre Balligand, Alex Barlow, Jean-François Bellemère, Stéphanie Bossé, the Bouchard family, Xavier Brun, Building Paris, Vincent Campredon, Audrey Camus, Élodie Capelle, Stéphane Chalmeau, Columbia University GSAPP, Pierre Dariel, Agnès and Bruno Decaris, Véronique Descharrières, Jean-Louis Destans, Michel Desvigne, the Établissement Public du Parc et de la Grande Halle de La Villette, the Familistère de Guise, Frédéric Forte, Galia, Anne-Sophie de Gasquet, Fabrice Hergott, the Institut National de l'Audiovisuel, Jakob + MacFarlane, Alexandre Labasse, Michèle Lamy, Julien Lanoo, Denis and Diony Lebot, Fanny Léglise, Yoann Legrand, Lunance, Jean-François Marcheguet, Jean-Luc Martinez, Miguel Mazeri, Clarisse Mazoyer, Luca Merlini, Frédéric Migayrou, Myr Muratet, the Musée d'Art Moderne de Paris, the Musée du Louvre, the Musée National de la Marine, OPPIC, Michel Ouary, Frédéric Panni, Paris Habitat, the Pavillon de l'Arsenal, Éric and Marie-Pierre Plumet, Antoine Pradels, the Besançon Education Authority, Benoît Santiard, Caroline Santiard, Hélène Schwoerer, Ellie Stathaki, the Familistère Godin Joint Association, Bernard Tschumi, Ilan Urroz, Laurent Vallet, the City of Paris and its Construction, Heritage and Architecture Division, Wallpaper*.

Remerciements

Charlotte Hubert, Jean-Jacques Hubert et Antoine Santiard remercient tous les collaborateurs d'h2o architectes pour leur énergie. Ils remercient également pour leur confiance : Bruno Airaud, Artefactory, l'Assemblée nationale, Julien Attard, Jean-Pierre Balligand, Alex Barlow, Jean-François Bellemère, Stéphanie Bossé, la famille Bouchard, Xavier Brun, Building Paris, Vincent Campredon, Audrey Camus, Élodie Capelle, Stéphane Chalmeau, Columbia University GSAPP, Pierre Dariel, Agnès et Bruno Decaris, Véronique Descharrières, Jean-Louis Destans, Michel Desvigne, l'Établissement public du parc et de la grande halle de La Villette, le familistère de Guise, Frédéric Forte, Galia, Anne-Sophie de Gasquet, Fabrice Hergott, l'INA, Jakob + MacFarlane, Alexandre Labasse, Michèle Lamy, Julien Lanoo, Denis et Diony Lebot, Fanny Léglise, Yoann Legrand, Lunance, Jean-François Marcheguet, Jean-Luc Martinez, Miguel Mazeri, Clarisse Mazoyer, Luca Merlini, Frédéric Migayrou, Myr Muratet, le musée d'Art moderne de Paris, le musée du Louvre, le musée national de la Marine, l'OPPIC, Michel Ouary, Frédéric Panni, Paris Habitat, le Pavillon de l'Arsenal, Éric et Marie-Pierre Plumet, Antoine Pradels, le rectorat de Besançon, Benoît Santiard, Caroline Santiard, Hélène Schwoerer, Ellie Stathaki, le syndicat mixte du familistère Godin, Bernard Tschumi, Ilan Urroz, Laurent Vallet, la Ville de Paris et la Direction de la construction, du patrimoine et de l'architecture, Wallpaper*.

Editorial conception
Building Paris with h2o architectes
and Fanny Léglise

Graphic design
Building Paris
(Benoît Santiard, Guillaume Grall,
Cécile Legnaghi)

Photographs
Julien Attard
(p. 69-73, 77-78, 144-147, 151-152,
157-159, 171-172, 232-236, 264)

Stéphane Chalmeau
(p. 46, 48, 100-112, 116, 122, 130-143, 155,
174, 180-192, 197-207, 222, 225, 227, 228-229,
239-240, 244-246, 251, 252, 256, 258)

Julien Lanoo
(p. 210, 214-216, 220)

Julien Lelièvre
(p. 17, 33-34, 38-45, 51-65, 88-91, 148, 280-
282, 287-290, 296-304, 308-310, 313, 317-320)

Myr Muratet
(p. 75, 92-97, 118-121, 125, 162-167,
173, 175-176, 260, 263, 266)

h2o architectes
(p. 36, 81-86, 168-169, 194-195,
212-213, 248, 293-294)

English translation
John Tittensor

Proofreading
Raphaëlle Roux

Typefaces
Akzidenz Grotesk Next
(Berthold Type, 2006)
Lyon Text (Commercial Type)

Photo-engraving
Fotimprim, Paris

Papers
Munken Print White 80 g/m²
Magno Satin 100 g/m²

Conception éditoriale
Building Paris avec h2o architectes
et Fanny Léglise

Conception graphique
Building Paris
(Benoît Santiard, Guillaume Grall,
Cécile Legnaghi)

Photographies
Julien Attard
(p. 69-73, 77-78, 144-147, 151-152,
157-159, 171-172, 232-236, 264)

Stéphane Chalmeau
(p. 46, 48, 100-112, 116, 122, 130-143, 155,
174, 180-192, 197-207, 222, 225, 227, 228-229,
239-240, 244-246, 251, 252, 256, 258)

Julien Lanoo
(p. 210, 214-216, 220)

Julien Lelièvre
(p. 17, 33-34, 38-45, 51-65, 88-91, 148, 280-
282, 287-290, 296-304, 308-310, 313, 317-320)

Myr Muratet
(p. 75, 92-97, 118-121, 125, 162-167,
173, 175-176, 260, 263, 266)

h2o architectes
(p. 36, 81-86, 168-169, 194-195,
212-213, 248, 293-294)

Traduction anglaise
John Tittensor

Relecture
Raphaëlle Roux

Typographies
Akzidenz Grotesk Next
(Berthold Type, 2006)
Lyon Text (Commercial Type)

Photogravure
Fotimprim, Paris

Papiers
Munken Print White 80 g/m²
Magno Satin 100 g/m²

Printed in June 2020
by Musumeci in Quart (Italy)

Park Books
Niederdorfstrasse 54
8001 Zurich, Switzerland
www.park-books.com

Park Books is being supported by the Federal Office of Culture with a general subsidy for the years 2016–2020.

All rights reserved. No part of this publication may be reproduced, stored in a retrieval system or transmitted in any form or by any means, electronic, mechanical, photocopying, recording, or otherwise, without the prior written consent of the publisher.

© 2020, h2o architectes, Paris,
and Park Books AG, Zurich.
© For the texts, the authors.
© For the photographs, Julien Attard, Stéphane Chalmeau, Julien Lanoo, Julien Lelièvre, Myr Muratet, h2o architectes.

ISBN 978-3-03860-198-2

Achevé d'imprimer en juin 2020 sur
les presses de Musumeci à Quart (Italie)

Park Books
Niederdorfstrasse 54
8001 Zurich, Suisse
www.park-books.com

La maison d'édition Park Books bénéficie d'un soutien structurel de l'Office fédéral de la culture pour les années 2016-2020.

Tous droits réservés. La reproduction, traduction ou adaptation totale ou partielle de cet ouvrage, sous quelque forme que ce soit et par quelque procédé que ce soit, est strictement interdite sans l'autorisation expresse préalable de l'éditeur.

© 2020, h2o architectes, Paris,
et Park Books AG, Zurich.
© Pour les textes, les auteurs.
© Pour les photographies, Julien Attard, Stéphane Chalmeau, Julien Lanoo, Julien Lelièvre, Myr Muratet, h2o architectes.

ISBN 978-3-03860-198-2